CHILDREN OF POVERTY

Studies on the Effects
of Single Parenthood,
the Feminization of Poverty,
and Homelessness

edited by

STUART BRUCHEY
University of Maine

A GARLAND SERIES

WELFARE REFORM

HELPING THE LEAST FORTUNATE
BECOME LESS DEPENDENT

RICHARD L. KOON

GARLAND PUBLISHING, INC.
NEW YORK & LONDON / 1997

Library of Congress Cataloging-in-Publication Data

Koon, Richard L., 1947–
    Welfare reform : helping the least fortunate become less
dependent / Richard L. Koon.
        p.   cm. — (Children of poverty)
    Includes bibliographical references and index.
    ISBN 0-8153-2799-4 (alk. paper)
    1. Public welfare—United States. 2. Welfare recipients—
Employment—United States. 3. Job Opportunities and Basic Skills
Training Program (U.S.) I. Title. II. Series.
HV95.K65 1997
361.6'8'0973—dc21   96-49747

Printed on acid-free, 250-year-life paper
Manufactured in the United States of America

*For my parents, William and Mary Koon, who
have always stressed the importance
of a good education.*

Contents

Appendices

List of Tables

x

Charts

xiii

Preface

It was six men of Indostan
To learning much inclined,
Who went to see the Elephant
(Though all of whom were blind),
That each by observation
Might satisfy his mind.
   —John G. Saxe, "The Blind
   Men and the Elephant"

Since its inception in the 1930s, AFDC has been a controversial and much criticized federal program. When people talk about welfare and the problems associated with the welfare system, AFDC is usually the program they are talking about. There are approximately 4.5 million families currently receiving public assistance payments in the form of Aid to Families with Dependent Children (AFDC). The vast majority of all AFDC recipients are single mothers with an average of two children, and most AFDC families receive little or no assistance from the children's fathers. Many women who head the families have been victims of abuse and often lack an education, job skills, or meaningful work experience. There are significant barriers between these women and a good job that will allow them to support their families without some government assistance.

Like the proverbial six learned blind men who went to study the elephant, however, few people really study and view the AFDC system in its entirety. They tend to observe only parts of the system, and their view tends to be myopic, often shaded by ignorance, and frequently based on the "welfare stereotype."

xv

> The First approached the Elephant,
> And happening to fall
> Against his broad and sturdy side,
> At once began to bawl:
> "God bless me! but the Elephant
> Is very like a wall!"

> The Second, feeling of the tusk,
> Cried, "Ho! what have we here
> So very round and smooth and sharp?
> To me 'tis mighty clear
> This wonder of an Elephant
> Is very like a spear!"

Many observers focus on the negative aspects of the public welfare system, viewing it as a socialistic program that encourages dependency on the government by providing an alternative to work. Why, they ask, will people work in low-paying, entry-level jobs, when they can collect a package of public assistance benefits that will equal or almost equal what they would earn from working? These observers also question whether it is fair for many people, including single mothers with children, to work in entry-level, low-paying jobs, while others choose to receive public assistance. For certain observers this is one of the most onerous characteristics of the welfare system, though its degree of prevalence is arguable.

> The Third approached the animal,
> And happening to take,
> The squirming trunk within his hands,
> Thus boldly up and spake:
> "I see," quoth he, "the Elephant
> Is very like a snake!"

These observers note that the public welfare system encourages long-term welfare dependency. After all, we occasionally hear stories of multiple generations from the same family living on public assistance: Families where the grandmother started receiving welfare, her teen-age daughter had a child and received welfare, and now her daughter's teenager is having a child and receiving welfare. Frequently, the public perceives that welfare has become more than just a way of life for people, that in some families, it has become a tradition. All too often it appears, people are having children to collect welfare and avoid working. Yet, while this phenomenon occurs in the welfare system, its extent is also questionable.

> The Fourth reached out his eager hand,
>   And felt about the knee,
> "What most this wondrous beast is like
>   Is mighty plain," quoth he;
> " 'Tis clear enough the Elephant
>   Is very like a tree!"

Additionally, observers of the welfare system point out that the system has branched out in its effects, possibly creating a "culture of poverty"—that is, an underclass of individuals whose values deviate distinctly from societal norms. These observers feel this deviant culture exists primarily in the inner cities, and is characterized by, among other things, a high degree of public assistance utilization; low work ethic; low educational attainment as represented by large high school dropout rates; high rates of unwed births, especially to teenagers; high rates of substance abuse; and heightened criminal activity. Again, while some people using public welfare belong to this "culture of poverty," most do not. Whether this view of welfare is valid depends a great deal on the ideology of the observer.

> The Fifth, who chanced to touch the ear
>   Said, "E'en the blindest man
> Can tell what this resembles most;
>   Deny the fact who can,
> This marvel of an Elephant
>   Is very like a fan!"

Still other observers focus on the positive aspects of the public welfare system and discourage viewing welfare from commonly perceived stereotypes. Those with this perspective point out that in a majority of instances, AFDC accomplishes its intended purpose of providing a temporary safety net for families who lose their means of support through death, divorce, or abandonment. These observers note that even though the proportion of unwed mothers receiving AFDC has increased since its inception, the overriding function of the welfare system has been to encourage economic and family stability. Facts substantiate the existing system provides a minimum level of support, which keeps families together until they can get on their feet again. Data indicate most recipients do not become welfare dependent; in fact, the average AFDC recipient receives assistance for less than two years. In addition, research indicates that while receiving welfare, many parents participate in education, job training, or educational programs expressly aimed at decreasing their dependence on the welfare system.

> The Sixth no sooner had begun
> About the beast to grope,
> Than, seizing on the swinging tail
> That fell within his scope,
> "I see," quoth he, "the Elephant
> Is very like a rope!"

Sympathetic observers of the welfare system point out that regardless of the system's faults—and they admit it has many—the system exists mainly to support children. Despite rhetoric that implies otherwise, the only way people receive AFDC benefits in America is when they have children and no resources to support their children. These observers concede some parents who receive welfare could be working. But that is not their children's fault. Some children have parents who have made unsound decisions like dropping out of school, having a child too early, or abusing drugs or alcohol. These observers question if society should really hold the child responsible for the actions of the parent.

> And so these men of Indostan
> Disputed loud and long,
> Each in his own opinion
> Exceedingly stiff and strong.
> Though each was partly in the right,
> And all were in the wrong!

Just as loudly, the United States continues to debate the future of its public welfare system. In the 1992 presidential election, President Clinton promised to "end welfare as we know it." In the 1996 elections, welfare was a major policy issue at both state and national levels. Significant changes were enacted at the federal level in August 1996, three months before the November general election. These revisions in national policy center around ending the entitlement status of AFDC by giving the states a block grant and letting each state set its own rules, within new federal guidelines. Most policy experts would consider this move as "changing the welfare system as we know it," but others view this proposal as the federal government washing its hands of a problem, which it has failed to deal with successfully, by giving the problem to the states.

Prior to the new welfare reform legislation, the Clinton administration has allowed states to experiment with welfare reform on a smaller scale by granting states "1115 Waivers," or permission to deviate from federal rules and regulations so states can conduct welfare reform experiments. State experiments include innovations such as providing limits on how long a family can receive AFDC; requiring mandatory work or job-training participation; requiring teen-age parents to live with their parents; grant capping, or not raising the grant amount if an AFDC recipient has an additional child while receiving benefits; and allowing families to keep more earnings and acquire additional assets without losing AFDC eligibility completely (the concept of permitting families to work their way off welfare gradually). However, many of the state 1115 Waivers or experiments merely complement state programs funded by the Family Support Act of 1988 (FSA), Job Opportunities and Basic Skills Training Program (JOBS), Public Law 100-485.

As block grants become a reality, the new federal legislation eliminates the JOBS program and allows the states to design their own welfare reform programs. JOBS funding, presently a capped entitlement, is now being merged with AFDC program funding and given to the states as one lump sum to administer as the states see fit, with certain federal strings attached.

Changing the welfare system presents both opportunity and risk— the opportunity to improve a flawed, sometimes counterproductive program that costs millions of taxpayer dollars, and the risk of damaging a system that millions of families depend on when they have nowhere else to turn for assistance. The question for the future is whether change will be based on a realistic assessment of the "whole elephant"—the entire system examined through rational analysis and evaluation—or whether change will result from viewing parts of the elephant, the parts that tend to make good sound bites while appealing to the perceived biases of voters.

This book provides background for evaluating public policy choices. It is based on my doctoral dissertation, completed in December 1993 at the University of Missouri-Columbia, and it has been revised and updated with an additional chapter reviewing developments in the area of welfare reform that have occurred since the time of the original publication. Though this book focuses on the state of Missouri's JOBS program, it incorporates and compares national data when possible, and it raises the same fundamental questions about the fate of welfare in this country.

Acknowledgments

First, I wish to acknowledge the contributions of the members of my doctoral committee. The committee was headed by Professor Dean Yarwood, who served as my dissertation advisor and provided insight, guidance, and encouragement over many years. His rigorous scrutiny of my work and many astute suggestions greatly contributed to the end product. In addition, I am grateful to Professors Richard Hardy, Gregory Casey, J. Kenneth Benson, and Scott Ward. Their input, comments, and encouragement added immeasurably to this study.

Also, I would like to thank some of my co-workers in the Missouri Department of Social Services, especially Carmen K. Schulze, director of the Missouri Division of Family Services, who allowed access to agency data and was very supportive during the entire process. I would also like to thank Michael Malaby and Mark Finnell for compiling the JOBS Research Data Set and for their assistance and advice. Further, I would like to thank staff from the Division of Family Services, especially FUTURES staff, who provided me with comments, suggestions, and information during many interviews.

My wife, Celeste, also receives exceptional thanks for her input. And I particularly want to thank my editor, Nancy Bedan, who spent countless hours making this manuscript clear, precise, and readable.

Welfare Reform

I

Introduction

Social scientists, through policy analysis, can go beyond the tasks of understanding and explaining phenomena and make direct contributions to the improvement of specific policies and processes.[1]

During the last two decades, policy studies within political science
have been increasing in number. As policy analysts Lawrence Mead and
Yehezkel Dror have noted, recent political science literature contains numerous "policy studies" in the sense that they focus on policy outputs as
opposed to the traditional focus of political science on input processes.[2]
According to Lawrence Mead:

Policy studies have arisen, most fundamentally, because of the policy problems of western governments
and the limited response to them by earlier political
science. In recent decades, these governments have
found it increasingly difficult to satisfy popular demands
for economic growth and benefit programs.[3]

In addition, policy analysts argue that the focus of policy studies
on outputs is a result of conflict within existing institutions over the proper
role of government, issues of government responsiveness, and the normative values associated with benefit programs.

This study focused on one of the most controversial of all governmental benefit programs, Aid to Families with Dependent Children
(AFDC), commonly referred to as "welfare." More specifically, this in-

vestigation examined the outcomes of government policies intended to reduce welfare dependency through the creation of education, employ-ment, and training programs for AFDC recipients.

THE POLICY PROBLEM

The Aid to Families with Dependent Children program, originally called Aid to Dependent Children and created by the Social Security Act of 1935, has been in existence for over sixty years. During much of its existence, AFDC has been the center of heated controversy. After all, President Roosevelt often referred to "cash relief" as a "narcotic," while President Lyndon Johnson stressed repeatedly that the object of his War on Poverty was to provide a hand up, not a handout. Much of the contro-versy centers around two issues: the proper role of government in public welfare policy and the effect of government policies on the behavior of individuals who receive public assistance.

As Irwin Garfinkel, a noted scholar on welfare policy, observes, American welfare policy is founded on four constraints: the belief that government is responsible for aiding the poor, the fear that such aid will create dependence, the distinction between groups of poor (such as the able-bodied and the elderly) in providing aid, and the community of val-ues.[4] These constraints have created a situation where the vast majority of welfare recipients are members of families headed by single women.

What makes this situation important is the fact that one-half of all children born in America will spend part of their childhood in a family headed by a mother who is divorced, separated, unwed, or widowed. About one-half of these families are headed by single women who are poor, and to some extent, dependent on welfare.[5]

Studies have shown that the mothers and children in such families tend to have poorer-than-average mental health and use a disproportion-ate share of community mental health services. Also, single mothers head-ing families dependent on welfare tend to have lower educational levels and lower self-esteem than women in two-parent families.[6]

Even more distressing is the fact that when compared to children who grow up in two-parent (husband-wife) families, the children from welfare families headed by a single mother are less successful on average when they become adults. These children are more likely to drop out of school, to give birth out of wedlock, to divorce or separate, to experience substance-abuse problems, to be involved with the criminal justice system, and to become dependent on welfare.[7] To exacerbate the problem, the number of children living in poverty families is increasing. In 1966, 17.6 percent of all children under eighteen years of age lived in poverty; presently this figure exceeds 21 percent. There is little optimism that this trend will reverse itself soon, since both the number of individuals living in poverty and the number of AFDC cases continue to grow. In federal fiscal year 1991, an average of 12,595,517 individuals received AFDC each month, the largest number in the history of the program. This included approximately 4.4 million adults, mainly single women, and an estimated 8.2 million children.[8]

During federal fiscal year 1991, AFDC benefits and administrative expenditures alone cost American taxpayers over thirty billion dollars. It is obvious that it is very expensive to allow large segments of the population to live on welfare. There are enormous costs associated with AFDC and other benefits such as Medicaid, public housing, mental health services, food stamps, and child care, in addition to collateral costs associated with substance abuse, child abuse, crime, and illiteracy.[9]

The American Public Welfare Association estimates that all levels of government spend over $225 billion a year on seventy-five separate public welfare programs and that approximately 4 percent of the total U.S. economy is devoted to public welfare. These figures do not include expenditures for middle-class assistance programs such as Social Security and Medicare.[10]

The role of government in addressing poverty and welfare dependency continues to be hotly debated and a source of acrimonious disagreement. As researchers such as Mead, Garfinkel, and McLanahan— among others—observe, much of the controversy centers around value conflicts that are associated with the individuals who belong to the poverty and welfare population.

Public policy reflects these value conflicts and thus often appears fragmented and disjointed. For instance, policymakers claim to support "family values" and strong families; at the same time, they enact legislation that discourages welfare mothers from marrying. Again, policymakers extol the virtues of work, but our public welfare laws and regulations contain provisions that discourage welfare recipients from working.[11]

Currently, government policy targeted at reducing welfare dependency is centered on the Family Support Act of 1988, Public Law 100–485, though the FSA is being replaced by the recently enacted Personal Responsibility and Work Opportunity Act of 1996. The Family Support

Act attempts to address the welfare problem in three ways. First, it includes changes in AFDC regulations in order to make it easier for AFDC recipients to go to work. Second, the FSA attempts to strengthen child support activities in order to make fathers or "absent parents" more responsible for supporting their children. Third, the FSA creates a new program to provide education, job training, and employment assistance to AFDC families through provisions of the Job Opportunities and Basic Skills Training Program (JOBS).[12]

The question is, will the Family Support Act succeed where other legislation and programs appear to have failed?

THE COMPLEXITY OF THE POLICY PROBLEM

Fixing the "welfare problem" has proved to be a persistently difficult task. Since the advent of the Great Society programs of the 1960s, there have been multiple programs targeted at helping people escape poverty thereby reducing the welfare roles. Some of the major programs included the Work Incentive Program (WIN) 1967–1989, Comprehensive Employment and Training Act (CETA) 1973–1981, and the Job Training Partnership Act (JTPA) 1981–present. In addition, numerous smaller programs such as Job Corps, Concentrated Employment Program (CEP), National Supported Work Demonstration, Negative Income Tax Experiments (NIT), and the Manpower Development and Training Act (MDTA) were created to provide education, job training, and job-search assistance to people living in poverty.

In many respects, these programs were probably successful at providing education and job-skills training to numerous individuals. In aggregate, however, these programs did not move a lot of people out of poverty and off welfare. After many years, the question still remains: Why haven't these programs accomplished more?

The issues associated with a person's decision to receive welfare are often complex, and are related to considerations such as individual values, societal structural factors, and economics. First, the value systems of individuals receiving AFDC are often questioned. After all, a significant portion of the women who receive AFDC drop out of school, have illegitimate children, and do not work. They have become members of what Martin Rein identified as the "culture of poverty."[13]

Research on the characteristics of AFDC mothers has consistently shown that recipients often exhibit attributes that present obstacles to employment. AFDC recipients tend to have young children in the home and to have a larger number of children than non-recipients.[14] These recipients are often substantially underschooled, have low job skills, and have had less successful work experience with fewer jobs and a lower rate of pay than the non-AFDC population.[15]

A second characteristic that has affected the outcome of programs is the culture of poverty concept. Proponents of the culture of poverty claim that poor people subscribe to a set of cultural values that are distinctive from and inferior to middle-class values. Rein's research supported this concept and found that many AFDC recipients attached little stigma to accepting welfare benefits. He concluded that their values contrasted with the "work ethic" of the upper and middle classes, which attaches a stigma to receiving welfare.[16] In a later study, however, Rein and Rainwater found that while the culture of poverty does exist, it was relevant only to approximately 20 percent of all AFDC mothers.[17] Greg Duncan and Saul Hoffman tend to support this estimate and found that approximately 30 percent of all AFDC mothers are heavily dependent on welfare as their main source of income.[18]

Opponents of the culture of poverty theory attribute class distinctions to differences in opportunities and experiences, not to value differences. Research by Linda Goodwin, Parham, and others tends to refute the culture of poverty theory.[19] Goodwin's research indicates that the poor and non-poor both share the same life goals and want to work. She concluded, however, that "the poor differ from non-poor in their experiences of success and failure, and that children who are born poor face discriminatory barriers to advancement in education and occupation. Failure in education and work reinforce psychological orientations that characterize the poor and discourage them from further work activity."[20]

Chrissinger found that while AFDC mothers aspired to middle-class income status and expressed a work ethic similar to members of the more general society, the extent of work activity of this group is determined by economic factors. It was the type of work available that determined how much they worked. Chrissinger also found that the need to care for young children prevented many AFDC mothers from working.[21]

A third factor affecting the success of previous programs is societal and economic structure. Several studies support the importance of economic and structural considerations in the decision to work or live on welfare. Research indicates that when AFDC mothers work, their jobs often are characterized by low status, low pay, high turnover, no fringe benefits, and no provisions for absence.[22] Research, however, indicates that welfare recipients continue to go to work despite the barriers they encounter. In reviewing the contributions of various types of income, Duncan and Hoffman found "the multi-year income of welfare families often contains more income from other sources than welfare. Much of the non-welfare income comes from the labor market."[23]

These seemingly contradictory findings demonstrate the complexity of the welfare dependency issue. Research indicates that personal characteristics and values, economic factors, and labor market considerations, all contribute to the problem of welfare dependency. Overall, an estimated 20–30 percent of AFDC families fall into the culture of poverty while the majority of families supplement AFDC with work, child support payments, and family assistance.

While some individuals are truly dependent on welfare for all of their support, others use AFDC benefits in much the same way that middle-class workers use occupational benefits—to lessen income insecurity and deficiency. Many AFDC mothers are in a transitional period attempting to cope with changes in circumstance, such as divorce or separation, widowhood, job loss, or illness. After all, numerous studies indicate that the majority of welfare mothers (50–66 percent) use benefits for short periods of time, two years or less. Fewer than 17 percent of all welfare recipients fall into the heavily dependent category.

The welfare rolls are very dynamic, reflecting considerable movement on and off welfare; at any point in time, however, approximately one-half of all mothers receiving AFDC fall into the heavily dependent category.[24] These single mothers and their children are the ones most likely to belong to the "culture of poverty" or what Kenneth Auletta calls the "underclass."[25]

METHODOLOGICAL ISSUES

A factor which contributes to the complexity of evaluating the welfare problem is the methodology used to study outcomes. It is difficult for policymakers to evaluate the short-term outcomes of education and job training programs particularly when the policymakers have not adequately defined program goals and when they have unrealistic expectations about the short-term potential of such programs to move people from welfare to work and out of poverty.[26] Considerable research indicates that employment and training programs targeted at welfare recipients often cost more to implement than they return in initial savings, as measured by increased earnings and reduced public assistance expenditures. In addition, some research questions the accuracy of using earnings and public assistance utilization as indicators of early program success.[27] Beyond this, research generally reveals that present programs do not move large numbers of people off of welfare and out of poverty.

The Manpower Development Research Corporation (MDRC) found that it may take up to five years before the typical employment and training program results in cost savings.[28] In fact, the real benefits from these programs may not occur for ten or twenty years and may be associated with the children of the individuals participating in current programs. These children may escape the culture of poverty due to their parents' participation in employment and training programs.

Another methodological issue associated with poverty intervention programs is the probability of determining with some degree of confidence that a program or strategy is having an actual effect. Can we know for certain that the individual who participates in a program and leaves welfare would not have left without the assistance of the program? MDRC has attempted to address this problem by using a classical experimental design to study employment and training program effects in several states; however, the MRDC experimental design mandates random assignment of participants to treatment and control groups. Many question the ethics of denying needy people government services because they are randomly assigned to a particular group.

A third methodological problem which complicates research about outcomes associated with the effectiveness of employment and training programs relates to the attributes of the group being studied. Welfare recipients tend to be suspicious of people asking questions about their situation. In order to receive public assistance, their life is literally placed under a microscope. They know that their eligibility for benefits and the benefit levels they receive will be affected by identification of income, unreported assets, or changes in family composition. In addition, many of the people receiving public assistance have literacy problems and do not respond well to traditional survey research methodology.[29]

The above discussion points out a few of the issues that contribute to both the complexity of the welfare problem and the study of the outcomes of programs which attempt to reduce welfare dependency. At this point, it is appropriate to question whether policymakers pay attention to the body of research concerning welfare recipients and welfare reform programs. It is also appropriate to ask if welfare reform policy is enacted based on the traditional stereotypes associated with the welfare population. For example, the mandatory nature of the current welfare reform legislation, combined with the "let's fix welfare" rhetoric being used by many political candidates, seems to focus more on the values and motivation to work of AFDC recipients than on the deterioration of employment opportunities for less-skilled workers. Also, much recent election year rhetoric indicates many candidates believe that present "welfare reform" programs are not producing significant positive outcomes.

THE 1990–1992 STUDY

This study examined the effectiveness of education, employment, and job-training programs at reducing an individual's dependency on the public assistance system. Specifically, it focused on the programs created by the federal Family Support Act of 1988, Job Opportunities and Basic Skills Training Program. While this study referenced national and various state-level data, it concentrated on the Missouri JOBS program, which was created to bring the state into compliance with federal JOBS legislation. We focused on specific outcomes of the JOBS program in order to provide an early assessment of the program's effectiveness at helping individuals reduce their dependence on welfare.

We presented several research questions and their related hypotheses for study and testing. Each of the research questions provided evaluative data concerning early outcomes of the JOBS program in Missouri. The principal research issue investigated by this study was as follows: Is the Missouri JOBS program doing what the Family Support Act intended—are JOBS participants reducing their dependency on the public assistance system? In addition, we attempted to identify specific JOBS activities that have an impact on reduced dependency, and whether there are individual attributes or geographic differences that appear to affect JOBS outcomes.

During the discussion about the complexity of the policy problem, several methodological issues were identified. The first issue raised, the ability to measure short-term program benefits using wages earned and AFDC benefits received as key indicators, is a problem inherent to research of this type and a problem for which this study did not adjust. The Missouri JOBS program had been in existence since July 1, 1990, and we only had data for two years at the time the study was conducted. The

MDRC studies indicate this time period is too short to evaluate the success or failure of an employment and training program based on increased wages and decreases in benefit amounts. Outcome data obtained after two years of program operation can, however, provide policymakers and program administrators with early indicators that programs either seem to be working or that there are problems.

Since 1960 Congress has created numerous programs such as the Work Incentive Program, Manpower Development and Training Act, Comprehensive Employment and Training Act, Concentrated Employment Program, negative income-tax experiments, and supported work experiments—which were in turn replaced by similar programs such as JTPA and JOBS.

Given this history, we question if elected officials have the patience to wait for long-term results, to withhold judgment before they declare a program is not working and reinvent the wheel. Yet, it is also questionable whether Congress or state legislatures will continue to support a multibillion dollar appropriation for the JOBS program without some indication that the program is having a positive impact.[30] The data obtained from early evaluations, while not definitive indicators of success or failure, can be compared with data from a previous period or with data from other states to provide relative indicators of early program effectiveness.

The second methodological issue, the ability to determine with a degree of certainty that the JOBS program is responsible for specific outcomes—that the outcomes did not occur by accident—was addressed in this study. Presently MDRC is using an experimental design to evaluate JOBS programs in several states. An experimental design, however, requires random assignment of subjects to the experimental and control groups, so some individuals who need and request JOBS services are denied services based on sampling protocols.

While experimental research designs are the ideal way to evaluate the experimental group effects of JOBS participation, experimental designs are not always practical in "real-life" administration. Missouri chose not to participate in the MDRC evaluations because of the ethical and political problems created when needy people are denied government services. To address this methodological issue, this study utilized a quasi-experimental design and compared the outcomes of an experimental group composed of individuals who participated in JOBS with the outcomes of a comparison group of AFDC recipients who have similar characteristics but who did not participate in JOBS.

A third methodological issue this study addressed is the problem of response bias associated with traditional survey research. The limitations of traditional survey research methodology with regard to bias introduced by both the subjects being studied and the investigator are well known. Theoretically, the response bias of subjects in this study could be even more problematic than normal because of their lower literacy levels and because of their perceived suspicions about people requesting information about their personal situations. These suspicions are often engendered by the regulatory aspects of welfare, which require recipients to provide detailed information about their income, assets, health, children, paternity of children, and personal relationships, including men that reside with female recipients. Because unreported income or assets, or even support from a family member, can reduce or obviate welfare benefits, recipients are often reticent about these matters. Moreover, welfare benefits can be reduced in some states if a child does not attend school regularly or if unmarried cohabitation occurs. In fact, many welfare recipients are subject to unannounced visits by staff from the local welfare agency to verify eligibility information—which further erodes the open communication needed for traditional survey research.

To control for this phenomenon, this study did not contact subjects, but obtained subject demographic and program outcome data from the administrative files of several state agencies that work with JOBS participants. For instance, data about participant characteristics, public assistance usage, and program outcomes are contained in the electronic data processing (EDP) files of the Missouri Department of Social Services, Division of Family Services (DFS). Data concerning wages earned, job referrals, and job entries are available from the EDP files of the Missouri Department of Labor and Industrial Relations, Division of Employment Security (DES).

In addition to examining the research questions posed later, we demonstrated the feasibility of using the large electronic data bases maintained by several governmental agencies to obtain participant outcome data. Data systems similar to the ones used in this study are available in almost every state as a potential source of valuable research data. The ability to obtain data concerning study subjects from administrative files minimizes some of the concerns associated with obtrusive measurement techniques utilized by traditional survey research.

In order to examine the early effectiveness of the JOBS program, this study presented seven research questions and their related hypotheses for inquiry and testing. It was anticipated that examination of the following questions would provide an early indication of the effectiveness of JOBS in Missouri and insight into whether JOBS is accomplishing the policy objectives of the Family Support Act.

Research Question 1: Are the most dependent AFDC recipients receiving JOBS employment and training services?

In order to minimize the "creaming" phenomenon, the Family Support Act requires that 55 percent of all JOBS resources be targeted toward three groups of AFDC recipients identified as being potentially the most dependent on welfare.

Question 1 examined the extent to which the Missouri JOBS program serves the most-dependent AFDC individuals.[31]

Research Question 2: Are JOBS participants representative of the AFDC population?

Much of the criticism associated with past employment and training programs for AFDC recipients involves the issue of "creaming" participants. This means that programs tend to work with the more motivated and less needy participants in order to achieve the highest possible success rates. Often the people in most need of services are not encouraged or required to participate. This question examined the extent of the "creaming" phenomenon in the JOBS program.

Research Question 3: Does JOBS participation result in increased labor force participation and decreased public assistance utilization?

Several studies have questioned the reliability of using wage effects or decreased AFDC utilization as reliable and unbiased indicators of the effectiveness of employment and training programs.[32] However, earned income and public assistance utilization continue to be the chief indicators of "perceived" success in most program evaluations. While there is a danger in placing too much reliance on these indicators, especially in a program that has been operating for only two years, it would be a greater danger to ignore the wage and welfare utilization indicators.

Wages earned and welfare benefits used are performance measures most policymakers consider meaningful.

Research Question 4: Which JOBS activities have the most impact on reduced AFDC dependency?

This question examined the activities that JOBS participants engage in to determine if particular activities are more likely than others to lead to employment and decreased AFDC utilization. There is considerable national debate concerning the most effective or optimum service delivery system. For instance, some analysts stress education activities as the best strategy to reduce dependency. Others argue that job-readiness and job-search activities are the most effective means of removing people from the welfare rolls.

Research Question 5: Are the people who successfully complete JOBS and enter employment different from the individuals who participate in JOBS and do not enter employment?

Question 5 attempted to identify individual characteristics that appear to have a bearing on successful program completion. There is a danger in identifying individual attributes that may predispose a person to success since identification may encourage selection of individuals who offer the greatest probability of success. However, these data are intended to provide an indicator of barriers that need to be overcome in order to have a higher probability of success.

Research Question 6: Is JOBS cost effective?

Question 6 examined JOBS program expenditures in relation to identifiable benefits or cost savings. As mentioned earlier, cost-benefit analysis of a new program is not an exact science. Research indicates that these types of programs often cost more in their early stages than they return in benefits. In addition, some of the benefits derived from welfare intervention programs are very difficult to measure and are beyond the scope of this study. We did, however, develop a cost-benefit analysis methodology to examine early program costs versus identifiable savings.

Research Question 7: Is there a significant difference in JOBS program outcomes for different geographic areas of Missouri?

Question 7 examined regional differences of JOBS participants, comparing the characteristics and outcomes of individuals in St. Louis, Kansas City, and southeast and northeast Missouri. While JOBS policy and procedures are guided by both federal and state regulations, JOBS allows for considerable local flexibility. For instance, the Kansas City JOBS program was designed by a committee of private sector community leaders who continue to exercise program oversight responsibilities. The St. Louis program was implemented without private sector input. This question will attempt to identify program outcome differences attributable to regional factors.

ORGANIZATION

This book is organized in what is intended to be a straightforward manner. Chapter 2 presents a historical review of public assistance in the United States and in Missouri, including a historical examination of anti-poverty programs, especially programs that were implemented specifically to target welfare recipients. This chapter also reviews some of the evaluation literature pertaining to major shifts or changes in U.S. public assistance policy and some of the key anti-poverty programs.

Chapter 3 examines the theoretical explanations for poverty, public assistance, and anti-poverty programs, which appear to have a bearing on public assistance policy in this country. It relies heavily on recent literature for much of its content.

In chapter 4 we review the Family Support Act of 1988, concentrating on the Job Opportunity and Basic Skills Training Program. This review focuses on the goals of the legislation and examines the features of this law that differ from similar past legislation. In addition, we identify specific desired policy outcomes that establish a foundation for inquiry into the research questions that follow. This chapter also briefly reviews the implementation of JOBS nationally, in Missouri, and in each of four sub-areas: St. Louis City, Kansas City-Jackson County, and several rural southeastern and northeastern Missouri counties. This section discusses demographic differences in each area and identifies different implementation strategies that may impact participant outcomes.

Chapters 5 and 6 are devoted to inquiry into the seven research questions posed earlier. Where appropriate, each chapter scrutinizes the research questions being asked and their related hypotheses from the national perspective, the state perspective, and the perspectives of the four regions being analyzed. State and local participant outcome data were obtained from the administrative data files of several Missouri state agencies. Comparable national data, where available, were obtained mainly from government documents and reports issued by the U.S. General Accounting Office, Office of the Inspector General for the Department of Health and Human Services, Family Assistance Administration of the Department of Health and Human Services, and the Manpower Demonstration Research Corporation.

Chapter 7 focuses on welfare reform activities which have occurred in recent years. This includes a review of the political debate taking place in Congress and an overview of the Personal Responsibility and Work Opportunity Act of 1996 (PRWO-96), which was passed by Congress and signed by President Clinton in August of 1996. Chapter 7 also provides a brief summary of current state welfare reform efforts and a review of the latest JOBS evaluation findings from the Manpower Demonstration Research Cooperation.

Throughout this book, especially in chapters 5 and 6, the emphasis is on an evaluation of the early outcomes of the JOBS program. The principal questions answered are whether the Missouri JOBS program accomplishes what the Family Support Act intended, and whether AFDC recipients who participate in JOBS activities reduce their dependency on the public assistance system.

This study is pertinent to both present and future policy regarding public assistance. As stated earlier, policy issues relating to welfare and welfare reform are now receiving considerable attention and will likely continue to be on the policy agenda for years to come. Congress enacted the Family Support Act of 1988, which has been heralded as landmark legislation, to initiate major changes in the country's welfare system. So far, all states have been required to make major changes in their AFDC and Child Support Enforcement programs and to administer an approved education and training program to combat welfare dependency. To further implement changes, Congress has amended the Job Training Partnership Act so resources will be redirected to assist the hard-to-serve unemployed—including welfare recipients.

In addition, while waiting for new federal legislation to become a reality, approximately forty states have gone ahead with welfare reform experiments after obtaining 1115 Waivers from the U.S. Department of Health and Human Services. These state experiments, many of which run in conjunction with and complement state JOBS programs, have helped define the Personal Responsibility and Work Opportunity Act of 1996 and will, in all likelihood, form the basis of state welfare reform strategies as states struggle to implement the new law. With passage of PRWO-96, the AFDC and JOBS programs end as entitlements, and funding for both programs is combined into a single block grant to the states. Theoretically, states will have considerable authority to design their own public assistance and welfare reform programs subject to the "attached strings" of the federal enabling legislation. At this point, an assessment of the recent changes and experiments is very important. Evaluation of welfare policy issues, especially issues relating to programs created by the Family Support Act and other reform initiatives, can provide an indication of whether national and state experiments are producing the desired results, thereby helping to focus future welfare reform efforts.

NOTES

1. David Paris and James F. Reynolds, *The Logic of Political Inquiry* (New York: Longman Inc., 1983), ix.

2. Lawrence M. Mead, "Policy Studies and Political Science," *Policy Studies Review* 5 (November 1985): 319–331. Also see Yehezkel Dror, "On Becoming More of a Policy Scientist," *Policy Studies Review* 8 (August 1984): 13–19.

3. Mead, "Policy Studies and Political Science," 319.

4. Irwin Garfinkel, "Welfare Policy In America," Institute For Research on Poverty, University of Wisconsin-Madison, Discussion Paper No. 847-87 (October 1987): 1.

5. Larry Bumpass, "Children and Marital Disruption: A Replication and Update," *Demography* 21 (February 1984): 71–82.

6. Irwin Garfinkel and Sara S. McLanahan, *Single Mothers and Their Children: A New American Dilemma?* (Washington, D.C.: Urban Institute, 1986), chap. 2.

7. Garfinkel, "Welfare Policy in America," 1–2.

8. U.S. Department of Health and Human Services, Information Memorandum No. ACF-IM-92-7 (May 21, 1992): Table TT1, 2.

9. Ibid., Table TT2, 5.

10. Richard Firrara, American Public Welfare Association, telephone interview with author, 15 June 1992.

11. For example, many states did not allow two-parent families to receive AFDC until they were required to by the Family Support Act of 1988. See section 401, Public Law 100–485.

12. U.S. Congress, Family Support Act of 1988, Public Law 100–485.

13. Martin Rein, *Work or Welfare?* (New York: Praeger Publishers, 1974).

14. M.B Sanger, *Welfare for the Poor* (New York: Academic Press, 1979).

15. Ibid.

16. Rein, *Work or Welfare?*

17. Martin Rein and Lee Rainwater, "Patterns of Welfare Use," *Social Service Review* 52 (June 1978): 511–534.

18. Greg Duncan and Saul Hoffman, "The Use and Effects of Welfare: A Survey of Recent Evidence" (Paper presented at the conference on The Political Economy of the Transfer Society, Tallahassee,

Florida, November 1987), 3–7.

19. L. Goodwin, *Do the Poor Want to Work?* (Washington, D.C.: Brookings Institution, 1972).

20. Ibid., 33.

21. M.S. Chrissinger, "Factors Affecting Employment of Welfare Mothers," *Social Work* 25 (October 1980): 52–56.

22. Sanger, *Welfare for the Poor*, 54.

23. Duncan and Hoffman, "The Use and Effects of Welfare: A Survey of Recent Evidence," 3.

24. Ibid., 5.

25. Kenneth Auletta, *The Underclass* (New York: Random House, 1982).

26. John H. Bishop, "Toward More Valid Evaluations of Training Programs Serving the Disadvantaged," *Journal of Policy Analysis and Management* 8 (1989): 209–228.

27. Ibid., 210–212.

28. Judith M. Gueron and Edward Pauly, *From Welfare to Work* (New York: Russell Sage Foundation, 1991), 32–39.

29. Greg Vadner, Deputy Director of Income Maintenance, Missouri Department of Social Services, Division of Family Services, interview with author, 17 June 1992.

30. Job Opportunities and Basic Skills Training Program, U.S. Department of Health and Human Services, 45 CFR Part 205 (October 13, 1989). See section 250.70–250.78.

31. Job Opportunities and Basic Skills Training Program, U.S. Department of Health and Human Services, 45 CFR Part 205 (October 13, 1989). See section 250.74 (a) (1).

32. Bishop, "Toward More Valid Evaluations of Training Programs Serving the Disadvantaged," 209.

II

Welfare and Welfare Reform:
The Historical Perspective

Mrs. Day's husband died in 1933, leaving her a widow with six children, the youngest a baby. The family had been forced to live in destitution.

Complaints from the school teachers were numerous. Threats were made by the neighbors to remove the children from the home. Mrs. Day was more interested in new permanents, beads, and gaudy clothing than whether her children attended school properly clothed. Clothing was contributed from various sources, but due to bad management, and lack of care, the children often attended school barefooted in winter.

When the application for aid to dependent children was first investigated, the home was in a deplorably filthy condition. No dishes were owned, and the corners of the table still indicated that members of the family had been served with water gravy on the bare table. The house was used as a shelter for chickens and dogs.

When Mrs. Day was accepted for aid to dependent children in July 1938, it was explained to her that much improvement would be expected. Frequent home visits were made and her buying was supervised. With the added means of support (the grant was $22), Mrs. Day entered into the spirit of maintaining a higher standard of living for herself and her family. With suggestions from the visitor, the house was rearranged and made more livable. Curtains and shades, linoleums, and a stove were purchased. Each child was equipped with a lunch box for school and clothes similar to those of other children.

At Christmas time, when the children were in an operetta at school, their appearance revealed such a decided change that many favorable comments were made.

Instead of complaints from school teachers and neighbors, Mrs. Day received the following note from one of the teachers: "I want to tell you how proud I am of Elsa. She is doing much better this year. Each morning she comes to school happy and clean and studies hard during the day. I think I have never seen a greater change in anyone and I certainly hope she continues this way."[1]

PRE-DEPRESSION PUBLIC ASSISTANCE POLICY

Assisting the unfortunate has been recognized as an important, and often controversial, government responsibility since the founding of America. Just as the early colonists continued to observe numerous other English traditions, they carried on the tradition of the English "poor law." Elizabethan Poor Law consisted of a system of local parish relief funded by local taxes. This system provided cash and in-kind assistance to those not expected to work and assisted the able-bodied with the raw materials to make goods for sale. By the eighteenth century, this system had evolved into a system of workhouses where the unemployed lived and worked at various tasks.[2]

By 1789, public assistance was one of the largest items of expenditure in many American cities; however, in the nineteenth century, responsibility for providing aid to certain groups of poor gradually began shifting to state governments. States commenced programs to care for the blind and insane, and to provide free public education funded by local property taxes. By mid-century, the federal government began to provide some assistance to disabled veterans of the Civil War, their widows and orphans, and some aid to former slaves.[3]

In the early twentieth century, the trend toward state assumption of responsibility for caring for the poor accelerated. Wisconsin enacted the first workmen's compensation law in 1908. By 1930, most states had workmen's compensation programs, more than half had widows' pension programs, and several had aid for the aged programs. In 1932, Wisconsin and New York enacted the first unemployment compensation programs.[4] Missouri had the distinction of enacting the first mother's aid law in the United States in 1911. In fact, the Missouri law was enacted prior to the 1913 establishment of a state agency responsible for dependent and neglected children.[5]

AID TO FAMILIES WITH DEPENDENT CHILDREN— THE CONTEMPORARY FRAMEWORK

Prior to the Great Depression and the Social Security Act of 1935, public assistance was considered the responsibility of state and local governments and private organizations. The Great Depression in the 1930s precipitated a dramatic shift in responsibility for financing and administering public assistance programs. The federal government's involvement in providing welfare income began with the goal of providing a means of subsistence for a large segment of the population that otherwise had none. According to Anna Kondratas, a Schultz senior policy analyst with the Heritage Foundation, "Welfare was a substitute for, not an alternative to, the labor market, because for many there was no labor market. The Aid to Dependent Children program, moreover, was initially to benefit widows, who were not expected to be in the labor market and whose lack of a means of support for children was beyond their control."[6]

When the Aid to Dependent Children program (ADC), was enacted in the 1930s, 88 percent of the families that received benefits were needy because the father had died. Their stories were similar to that of Mrs. Day, whose plight was described earlier. In 1949, 42 percent of the fathers of children on ADC were dead. By 1963, however, only 6 percent of the fathers of children on AFDC were deceased, and only 2.6 percent were deceased in 1977. By 1977, over 80 percent of the families on AFDC consisted of divorced, separated, deserted, or unmarried parents, with most of the remainder having incapacitated and unemployed fathers.[7]

Since the Great Depression, the nature and emphasis of welfare in this country has gradually shifted from a substitute for work that does not exist, to a supplement for low earnings and an alternative to work.[8] According to Kondratas:

The Aid to Families with Dependent Children program has changed in character. The vast majority of the 3.5 million poor women who head households—households in which more than half of the nation's poor children live—are not widows but divorced, separated, or never-married women, and most of them are on welfare.[9]

Prior to the 1960s, women with children were generally considered unemployable since a woman's place was considered to be in the home caring for her children. In recent years, however, women have entered the labor force in unprecedented numbers. The rationale for excluding able-bodied welfare mothers from labor-force participation is now questioned, especially when the majority of non-welfare mothers with children are in the labor force.

One recent study found that about half the women employed outside the home perceive that working is a matter of economic necessity for them, rather than a matter of choice.[10] Yet, some mothers are still choosing welfare instead of entering the labor market. As a result, the situation has developed where women with children who feel compelled to work are paying taxes to support the "preferences" of other women with children who choose to stay home.[11]

This changing perception of the role of women in the labor market has led to changes in the administration of the AFDC program. Between 1935 and 1962, the federal government did not stress work requirements in return for welfare benefits. In fact, work requirements in return for AFDC benefits were prohibited prior to 1962.

A major change occurred in 1962 when Congress instituted social services for the stated purpose of preparing welfare recipients for work. Yet, Mildred Rein, a noted authority on U.S. social policy, observes that despite the clear emphasis on work efforts and self-sufficiency for AFDC benefits and directing the AFDC recipient back to the labor market, no real effort was made to change program direction as a result of the 1962 law.[12]

EARLY ATTEMPTS AT WELFARE REFORM

Attempts to increase labor market participation and reduce welfare dependency took two approaches subsequent to 1962. The first approach consisted of work incentives. In 1967, changes to the Welfare Amendments decreased the effective tax on the earnings of AFDC recipients by instituting exemptions for the first thirty dollars in earnings and for one-third of all additional income. Rein noted that "in spite of increased employability of AFDC mothers, the national data show that work effort, as measured by those at work while on welfare and cases closed for employment, did not increase after the institution of the thirty and one-third earnings disregard."[13]

Later, the Omnibus Budget Reconciliation Act of 1981 (OBRA) drastically reduced work incentives by instituting a seventy-five-dollar flat work-related expense deduction and eliminating the thirty dollar and one-third provision after four months. In effect OBRA established two nominal tax rates on the earnings of AFDC recipients: 67 percent during the first four months of earnings and 100 percent thereafter.[14] According to Robert Moffitt, an economist who specializes in analyzing the labor-supply effects resulting from changes in government income transfer policy, "OBRA increased the tax rate back to 100 percent, the level prevailing prior to 1967. In retrospect, it appears that 1967 marked the end, not the beginning, of legislative progress on work incentives in the welfare system."[15]

With regard to the 1981 OBRA changes, Moffitt concluded, "The weight of the evidence implies that higher transfer-program tax rates such as those resulting from OBRA will reduce the work effort among the female-head population, and that lower tax rates would increase it."[16]

In contrast to Moffitt's findings, however, a 1984 U.S. General Accounting Office (GAO) report found that "most earners who lost AFDC benefits did not quit their jobs and return to AFDC." Also, the GAO concluded that "working AFDC recipients were no more likely to stop working and increase their reliance on AFDC after OBRA's implementation than they were in the prior year."[17] The GAO concluded that even though AFDC recipients endured financial hardships significantly more often after OBRA than in the years before it was passed, their work efforts were apparently not affected by the withdrawal of financial work incentives.[18]

The Deficit Reduction Act of 1984 (DRA), also contained provisions that might have an impact on the work effort of AFDC recipients. DRA increased each state's AFDC eligibility standard from the OBRA— 150 percent of each state's standard of need—to 185 percent of the state's standard of need. In addition, working AFDC recipients were allowed to keep thirty dollars of their monthly earnings for one year. The impact of DRA on the labor force participation of AFDC recipients has been inconclusive.

The second approach used to increase labor force participation among AFDC recipients consisted of mandatory and voluntary work requirements. As stated earlier, federal involvement in welfare since 1935 had never stressed work requirements; although Kondratas notes, many states had continued work requirements for some recipients of state-funded general assistance. In 1977, even after enactment of federal welfare programs, nineteen states still enforced work requirements in their general assistance programs.[19]

EARLY WELFARE EMPLOYMENT AND TRAINING PROGRAMS

Federal welfare-to-work initiatives had their beginning with the 1962 AFDC amendments which authorized the Community Work and Training Program (CWTP). CWTP allowed states to require AFDC recipients to work off their benefits. Only thirteen states, however, chose this option by the time the legislation expired in 1967. The less-than-enthusiastic reception of CWTP is often attributed to ambivalence on the part of elected officials as well as the ideological opposition of the social services professionals authorized to implement the changes.[20]

The 1967 AFDC amendments created the Work Incentive Program (WIN), the first federal mandate requiring "all" employable AFDC recipients to work or train for work. The initial focus of WIN was on job training, but in 1971 this focus shifted to job search and immediate employment. As Rein notes, however, the requirement for recipients to actively seek work stemmed not from a policy to discourage dependency, but from the view that employment was just another "service" available to AFDC recipients. The attitude of caseworkers toward mandatory work for AFDC mothers continued to be negative.[21]

Funding for WIN decreased steadily after the enactment of OBRA in 1981, and states were encouraged to replace the traditional WIN program with WIN demonstration programs. WIN demonstration projects allowed states greater flexibility in their use of WIN funds, and program administration rested solely with the state welfare agency instead of being split between the welfare agency and the state employment service. WIN demonstrations usually offered a mixture of components such as education, job search, work experience, and on-the-job training.

In addition to allowing WIN demonstrations, OBRA tightened eligibility for AFDC and reduced work incentives; it also permitted states to establish "workfare" programs under the Community Work Experience Program (CWEP), to make participating welfare recipients more employable. CWEP, commonly referred to as workfare, required AFDC recipients to work in unpaid employment designed to serve a useful and public purpose, but it did not require them to work in public-sector employment.

The CWEP programs and WIN demonstrations comprised the bulk of the workfare and work-related welfare reform initiatives aimed at increasing labor market participation and decreasing dependency among the AFDC population prior to the implementation of JOBS. Thirty-seven states experimented with these programs, though fewer than ten had statewide programs.[22] By 1990, however, WIN was eliminated entirely and replaced with the Job Opportunities and Basic Skills program, JOBS.

WORK FOR WELFARE: A REVIEW OF RECENT LITERATURE AND EMPIRICAL RESEARCH

Considerable literature and research is available concerning the topic of labor force participation and welfare dependency among AFDC recipients. Some early studies concerning labor force participation evaluated the effects of varying tax rates on the earnings of low-income individuals and income-maintenance recipients during the Negative Income Tax (NIT) experiments of the late 1960s and 1970s. These studies assessed the impact of varying tax rates on labor supply responses.

Between 1968 and 1982, the U.S. government spent $225 million (in 1984 dollars), of which $63 million, or 28 percent, represented direct payments to families. The goal of the experiment was to determine how families would adjust their labor force participation in response to the NIT. The NIT experiment was viewed by many as a possible replacement for the complex network of social service delivery programs making up the existing welfare system. [23]

Philip Robins studied the NIT experiments conducted between 1968 and 1982 in New Jersey, Iowa, North Carolina, and in Gary, Indiana; Seattle, Washington; and Denver, Colorado. He referred to them as "the most ambitious policy research undertaking ever attempted," and noted that while numerous studies of the NIT experiments have been conducted in the past, his study focused on "providing the reader with a general sense of what was found, in the form of a consensus set of estimates of labor supply responses."[24]

Robins observed that the NIT experiments were geographically dispersed across the country and were conducted in both urban and rural settings. The experiments provided for the different treatment of subjects, with experimental group subjects receiving guaranteed incomes that varied from 50 to 140 percent of the poverty level. In addition, tax rates in the experiments fluctuated in relation to the guaranteed income level from 30 to 70 percent. That is, for every dollar earned above the income guarantee, a subject's additional income was reduced by 30–70 percent.

Robins found that despite the wide range of treatments and evaluation methodologies, the labor supply responses from the NIT experiments were remarkably consistent. On the average, husbands reduced labor participation by about the equivalent of two weeks of full-time employment. Wives and single female heads-of-households reduced their labor participation by about three weeks of full-time employment, while youth reduced their labor participation by about four weeks of full-time employment. Robins noted that because women and youth work fewer hours per year than do husbands, the effects on these groups are correspondingly much larger in percentage terms.[25]

In addition Robins found:

> In comparing structural model estimates across experiments, there is a remarkable consistency in the estimated substitution and income effects. When averaged across experiments, the substitution and income effects are quite similar to those obtained from non-experimental studies. In general, wives' substitution effects are more than double husbands' substitution effects, while income effects for both spouses are similar. Single female heads have substitution effects between husbands and wives, but their income effects are twice as large. The results suggest negative uncompensated wage elasticities (at the mean) for husbands and single female heads, and positive uncompensated wage elasticity for wives.[26]

Robins commented that the above findings reflect the relatively generous NIT program, which had an average income guarantee equivalent to the poverty line and a tax rate equal to 50 percent. This meant for every dollar earned, fifty cents was subtracted from the guaranteed income.

Economists Gary Burtless and Robert Haveman, provided a more in-depth analysis of one of the NIT experiments, the Seattle-Denver experiment. The Seattle-Denver experiment tested an average income guarantee of 115 percent of poverty and a marginal tax averaging 50 percent (there were eleven different treatments available in this experiment). In addition, the experiment provided rebates for taxes on earned income. About 80 percent of the enrolled families faced a break-even level that was more than one-and-a-half times the poverty threshold, and 50 percent faced a break-even more than twice the poverty level.[27]

The authors felt "the labor supply findings from Seattle-Denver were considered sufficiently important to affect the welfare reform proposals submitted by the Carter Administration." The Seattle-Denver experiment showed quite convincingly that the work incentive provided by NIT's low marginal tax rate was more than offset by the work disincentive effects caused by the higher overall transfers. For example:

> Simulations based upon the Seattle-Denver results demonstrated that replacement of the current welfare system and food stamp programs with a national NIT that has a guarantee equal to three-quarters of the poverty line and a marginal tax of 50 percent would reduce aggregate labor supply in two-parent families by about 1 percent. Labor supply in two-parent families with annual incomes below $5,000 would be reduced by more than 8 percent."[28]

The findings of the Seattle-Denver experiment indicated that it would cost the government $1.79 in transfer outlays to raise the net income of poor two-parent families by one dollar. "In other words, 44 percent of the net program costs of the NIT would be 'consumed' by breadwinners in the form of leisure."[29]

In addition, the experiment found that lowering work incentives in transfer programs by raising the marginal tax rate increased aggregate work effort. They attributed this rather perverse finding to the fact that while increases in the marginal tax rate reduced the work effort of transfer recipients, this effect was more than offset by increases in the work effort that occurs among those who lost benefits altogether.

Burtless and Haveman point out that if the objective of public welfare policy is to increase work effort, increases in AFDC tax rates might conceivably be justified by findings of the Seattle-Denver experiment. This conclusion, however, rests on the premise that the main objective of transfer policy is to encourage work effort, and not to raise the living standards of the poor in an equitable and efficient way. The authors conclude "that the Seattle-Denver experiment has played a useful role in overturning the notion, especially popular among economists and idealistic reformers, *that lower marginal tax rates are automatically associated with a greater stimulus to work.*"[30]

The Seattle-Denver experiment also included an interesting component to test the feasibility of issuing education and training vouchers to low-income family heads. Some of the experiment's subjects were randomly assigned to groups that were reimbursed for their education or training at a rate of either 50 percent or 100 percent. Participation in training, however, was voluntary.

Theoretically, this additional investment in training and education, or "human capital," should have improved the participants' employability and future earnings. The authors noted that participation in the voucher program was higher than anticipated. One-fifth of the family heads in two-parent families used the 50 percent vouchers, while one-third used the 100 percent vouchers. In contrast, about one-third of the single mothers who received 50 percent vouchers used them, as did almost one-half of those who were given 100 percent vouchers.[31]

According to Burtless and Haveman:

> The interesting finding from this experiment is the complete lack of evidence that the increased investment in schooling by participants led to any pay-off in the job market. On the contrary, persons eligible for vouchers—in comparison to control group members—suffered short-term reductions in wage rates, earnings, and employment during the initial phase of their eligibility. And they never showed consistent earnings gains over the entire six-year span for which information is available, a period which includes a fairly lengthy spell in which participants had completed their schooling.[32]

The authors offered the following explanations for these results. First of all, the amount of extra training was too small and the character of the extra training was not particularly relevant to the participants' labor market situation. In addition, the labor market was rather poor and generally deteriorating during the experiment. In such a labor market, the returns gained from work experience and job-keeping may exceed those gained from increased schooling. "It is difficult to make training pay off if there are few jobs available."[33]

In their study, *Labor Supply and Welfare Programs: A Dynamic Analysis*, Blau and Robins concluded their empirical results support previous research which shows welfare programs have a disincentive effect on labor supply. According to Blau and Robins, "Virtually all studies of this issue have examined work incentives within a static framework. The main conclusion drawn by these studies is that welfare programs create significant work disincentives. These work disincentives are identified as a reduction in either annual hours of work, the labor force participation rate, or the employment rate."[34]

The authors claimed that past studies paid little attention to the dynamic aspects of work disincentives and that recent studies have corrected this flaw by using qualitative choice theory to explain labor supply decisions over time. The dynamic models are natural extensions of static random utility qualitative choice models used frequently to analyze cross-sectional labor force data for a specific point in time.[35]

In conducting their study, Blau and Robins used Employment Opportunity Pilot Project (EOPP) household survey data for 29,620 families. This survey was conducted in 1980 in twenty geographically dispersed areas throughout the United States, and it collected information concerning employment and labor force participation for a sixteen-month to twenty-two-month period.

The authors found that with respect to EOPP participants, welfare programs influenced virtually every labor market movement, *but the biggest effects seemed to occur on transition rates into employment.* They also found the estimated effects on transition into employment existed for both welfare recipients and non-recipients, even when adjusted for differences in personal characteristics. Furthermore, the authors stated:

> For each group studied, welfare programs act to lengthen periods of time spent unemployed and periods of time spent out of the labor force. The effects are par-

ticularly large on periods of time spent unemployed, but it is conjectured that the job-search requirements of welfare programs may be creating a significant incentive for nonworkers to report themselves as being in that state.[36]

In addition, Blau and Robins noted:

Although the major effect of welfare programs appears to be on transition into employment, there are also significant effects on transitions out of employment. Here, the results differ considerably according to demographic group and whether adjustments are made for the effects of demographic group and whether adjustments are made for the effects of personal characteristics.[37]

After adjusting for the effects of personal characteristics, Blau and Robins found that single women on welfare exhibit significantly higher exit rates from employment to both unemployment and out-of-labor-force status; and that youths living in welfare families exhibit significantly lower exit rates from employment to unemployment and out-of-labor-force status. Also, men and married women on welfare have higher employment departure rates than their nonwelfare counterparts, although these effects are almost fully accounted for by their personal characteristics. For men and married women, the only transition rate from employment that was significantly higher among welfare recipients was the transition rate to unemployment for men. The authors felt that personal characteristics, rather than welfare status, accounted for the higher rates for loss of employment exhibited by welfare recipients.[38]

In addition, they identified several policy implications that include public efforts aimed at helping welfare recipients find jobs, and developing methods of improving job-search productivity either through direct support or through incentives for welfare recipients to improve their own job-search behavior.

Recent research concerning welfare recipients and their work efforts have concentrated on the experiences of the Work Incentive Program, WIN demonstration projects, Community Work Experience Programs, and other demonstration initiatives authorized by OBRA-1981. In 1986, twenty-four states were operating regular WIN programs, and twenty-six states were conducting WIN demonstration projects. In addition, thirty-seven states were operating AFDC community work experience programs, job-search programs, work supplementation programs, or special grant diversion demonstration programs.[39]

WIN was introduced in 1967 as a discretionary program, and became mandatory in 1971. WIN targeted employment and training services to the able-bodied AFDC recipient. As a condition of receiving AFDC benefits, all adult AFDC recipients who had no pre-school children or other barriers to employment were required to register with the state employment service, to participate in job training or job-search activities, and to accept employment offers.

In theory, WIN imposed a participation obligation, but it was never actually funded at a level adequate to create a "slot" for each able-bodied person—the precondition of a real work test.[40]

The general consensus concerning WIN's effectiveness was that WIN did not result in successful job placements for a significant number of clients. In spite of the large numbers of participants, one study indicated that in 1973, only 13 percent of AFDC family heads were involved in WIN, and of these, less than half were employed for at least ninety days immediately following their initial entry into employment.[41]

One recurring criticism of the WIN program was that it did not emphasize service to the long-term or "hard core" AFDC recipient. The more highly motivated volunteer AFDC participants were often favored in the selection process. One 1974 study of 4,700 WIN job placements found that this group was substantially different from the general AFDC population. The WIN workers who obtained employment were in their prime working years, fairly well educated, had good work histories, were in better health, and had been on welfare for relatively short periods. In other words, many of the WIN participants placed were job-ready prior to receiving WIN services and probably would have entered employment on their own without WIN assistance.[42]

In spite of WIN's limited overall success, a few particular program components and strategies were more effective than others. One major study found that work experience and vocational training for women, and on-the-job training and public service employment for both men and women had a greater effect on earnings than did more generic job placement assistance procedures. In general, the more intensive components such as work experience, vocational training, on-the-job training, and public service employment produced more positive results than just basic job-search assistance.[43]

According to Dickinson:

> High-performing WIN programs were distinguished
> from low-performing units by their use of intensive
> employment services and delivery techniques. For ex-
> ample, high performing programs provided job-search
> training and stressed clients' systematic, intensive job-
> search activities through groups or individualized coun-
> seling and follow-up. Low-performing units, however,
> paid little or no attention to providing either individual
> clients or groups with training in job search skills. These
> clients were told to apply for a certain number of jobs
> and to report back within a particular time period.[44]

The bottom line in WIN's failure to generate adequate numbers of
job placements was funding. Only 40 percent of all WIN-AFDC clients
received any service at all, and that service was typically job-placement
assistance—the least costly, but least cost-effective WIN component. As
a result, the WIN program was more of a registration requirement than a
work requirement.[45]

The 1981 Omnibus Budget Reconciliation Act allowed states to
assume greater authority for and flexibility in administering the WIN program. Under the OBRA WIN demonstration provisions, states were authorized to fund on-the-job-training programs by diverting recipients' welfare grants into wage subsidies for private employers. Twenty-seven states
eventually conducted WIN demonstration projects though little evaluative data exists concerning the effectiveness of their programs. The 1981
OBRA also authorized states to require AFDC recipients to work in public or nonprofit agencies in return for their welfare benefits under Community Work Experience Program provisions.

In addition, the Tax Equity and Fiscal Responsibility Act of 1982
(TEFRA) permits states to operate job-search programs for AFDC recipients. While TEFRA requires job-search programs to be implemented statewide, states have considerable flexibility in mandating who has to participate.

MANPOWER DEMONSTRATION RESEARCH CORPORATION: MULTISTATE PRE-JOBS EVALUATIONS

Recent multistate workfare studies of these various programs conducted by the Manpower Demonstration Research Corporation (MDRC) have concluded that "workfare works." While the results are not always dramatic, workfare states have a measurable increase in labor market participation by AFDC recipients. In general, workfare participants have increased earnings and reduced welfare dependency when compared to similar populations not participating in workfare programs.[46]

Employment rates for workfare participants were found to be 3 to 8 percent higher than for other welfare recipients. In addition, workfare alumni who found jobs generally increased their incomes; for example, one group increased incomes 36 percent over the control group.[47]

The 1981 OBRA allowed states considerable flexibility in design and administration of WIN demonstration and CWEP programs, and as a consequence, program components varied between states. Many of the programs deviated from the classic workfare model where the AFDC client is required to work a certain number of hours in return for a welfare grant. Some programs consisted of job-search activities, remedial education, institutional training, on-the-job training, and other programs aimed at increasing the clients' employability and prospects for long-term self-sufficiency. Approximately one-third of all CWEP participants at any one time were in a training activity rather than at a work site.[48]

Several state programs provided a mix of program components. Typically, a welfare recipient might initially be required to conduct a job search. If the job search was not successful, then the recipient might be required to participate in some type of employability training or to perform community service work. Most states did not require CWEP participants to work off their entire grant or to remain in the program for as long as they continued to be eligible for AFDC. In addition, CWEP participants were typically reimbursed for their work-related expenses.

Participation requirements for the various workfare programs differed from state to state. Only four states had statewide programs. In addition, many AFDC recipients were excluded from mandatory program participation. The most common exclusion was for the parents of children younger than age six. A 1984 U.S. General Accounting Office report found that most eligible AFDC recipients did not participate in CWEP programs. Of the sixteen states surveyed, only one, Alabama, had eligibility requirements allowing as many as half of its AFDC recipients to participate. No state had as many as 20 percent of its AFDC recipients actually participating in CWEP.[49] Similarly, MDRC found that few states clearly articulated a goal of full, or universal, participation.[50]

The MDRC research design addressed four basic questions concerning the effectiveness of future workfare feasibility and effectiveness. These questions are as follows:

Research Question 1: Is it feasible to impose obligations—or participation requirements—as a condition of welfare receipt?[51]

Pre-1981 OBRA WIN experience suggested that large-scale workfare was not feasible. MDRC findings indicated that in some circumstances it would be feasible to run a mandatory workfare program for a substantial segment of the AFDC caseload, although because of the diversity of the programs studied and their conflicting goals, MDRC urged caution in replicating large-scale mandatory programs in other states. MDRC identified the following factors as affecting program participation rates: prior staff experience, agency administrative capacity, staff attitudes, program philosophy, AFDC population demographic characteristics, and local conditions and resources.

MDRC concluded there is also uncertainty about the feasibility of an open-ended participation obligation imposed on the entire caseload, as proposed in the Reagan administration's 1985 Work Opportunities and Welfare legislation. Among the unknowns were the required levels of staff and funding, the feasibility of developing adequate program slots, and the extent of regular staff displacement by CWEP workers.

Research Question 2: What do workfare-type programs look like in practice, and how do welfare recipients themselves judge the fairness of mandatory requirements?[52]

MDRC found that most states did not design or implement CWEP with punitive intent. Moreover, 60–70 percent of the CWEP applicants considered the work requirement fair. In addition, MDRC found the jobs obtained by participants were generally entry-level positions in maintenance or clerical fields, parks, and human services. On the whole, the jobs did not provide substantial skill development because most of the participants had adequate working skills at the time they began work. Also, MDRC observed that while the work experience positions did not, for the most part, develop new job skills, they were not "make-work jobs." Supervisors judged the work important and indicated that participants' productivity and attendance were similar to those of most entry-level workers.

MDRC also found that a large proportion of the participants interviewed had positive feelings about their work assignments. They were satisfied with the positions, felt good about going to work, believed that they were making a useful contribution, and felt that they were treated as part of the regular work force. Many participants, however, believed that the employer got the better end of the bargain, or that they were underpaid for their work. In brief, they would have preferred a regular job. These results are consistent with the findings of prior studies that show that the poor want to work and are eager to take advantage of opportunities to do so.

Research Question 3: Do the state initiatives reduce the welfare rolls and costs and/or increase employment and earnings?[53]

MDRC found consistent, although relatively modest, employment gains. In interpreting the results, one should remember that the impacts, or program effects, are expressed as averages for a large segment of the caseload. Thus, even relatively small changes—multiplied by a large number of people—may have considerable policy significance.

In a three-state study, MDRC found that over the full follow-up period, average welfare payments to experimental group subjects were 8 percent or $288 per year less than the average payment to control group subjects. They also found that a program's impact on employment and earnings was greater if individuals who do not find employment in job-search workshops are required to meet a short-term work obligation. MDRC was not able to determine if the impacts were sustained or it they deteriorated over time.

Research Question 4: How do program benefits compare to program costs?[54]

Based on a study of three program sites, MDRC felt that society as a whole gained from all three programs. When the net impact on government budgets was considered, the following important insights are apparent. First of all, these programs often cost rather than save money. This reflects the fact that almost all of the costs are incurred up front although most of the benefits occur over time. Training is costly, but in time, participation leads to employment and earnings, which in turn lead to increases in the taxes the new workers pay, as well as reductions in their welfare benefits and related transfer programs.

In addition, MDRC found that under the funding formulas and matching agreements that were in place, the federal government bore more than half of the costs, but also enjoyed the greatest net savings. Without federal funds, states and counties would have had no financial incentive to run the programs. Gross operating costs per participant ranged from a low of $165 in Arkansas to a high of $1,050 in Maryland.

MDRC cautioned in its interim and later reports that the results of their studies warrant careful interpretation. First of all, MDRC points out that the findings, while generally positive, indicate the programs led to relatively modest increases in both employment and welfare savings. In addition, MDRC felt that differences among the states in the characteristics of the welfare population, local economic conditions, participation rates, AFDC benefit levels, and the extent of support services provided to program participants may impact the effectiveness of different program approaches. The MDRC research provides an indication, however, that welfare-to-work programs can produce positive benefits for both the program participant and possibly even the taxpayer.

In conclusion, since its inception in 1935, the Aid to Families with Dependent Children program has evolved from a plan designed to provide temporary assistance to a small number of widows and orphans into a primary source of income for many single mothers and their children. This unintended evolution of the AFDC system has resulted in numerous attempts by both federal and state governments to reform welfare and modify the behavior of AFDC recipients. These efforts have met with questionable success and have culminated in the multistate welfare-to-work demonstration projects authorized by OBRA-1981 and the present Family Support Act.

NOTES

1. Missouri State Social Security Commission, *Aiding Needy Persons in Missouri* (1939), 78–79.

2. Irwin Garfinkel and Robert Haveman, "Income Transfer Policy in the United States," *The Handbook of Social Intervention* (Sage Publications Inc.: 1983), 481–482.

3. Ibid., 481–482.

4. Ibid., 481–482.

5. Missouri State Social Security Commission, *Index of Public Assistance in Missouri* (1939), 319.

6. Anna S. Kondratas, "The Political Economy Of Work-for-Welfare," *Cato Journal* 6 (Spring/Summer 1986): 231.

7. Nancy Dickinson, "Which Welfare Strategies Work?" *Social Work* 31 (July/August 1986): 266.

8. Lawrence M. Mead, *Beyond Entitlement* (New York: The Free Press, 1986), 69.

9. Kondratas, "The Political Economy of Work-for-Welfare," 231.

10. Decision Making Information, *National Survey on Women's Issues* (McLean, Va.: 1983), 11.

11. Certainly "preference" is not the only factor involved in a woman's decision to choose welfare over the labor market. Economic considerations can have a large impact on this decision. Often a low-wage, secondary labor market job without medical benefits cannot provide the minimum level of economic subsistence the family needs. The welfare package—AFDC, Medicaid, food stamps, energy assistance, low-income housing, access to job-training and education programs, etc..— can often exceed the income available from a minimum-wage job.

12. Mildred Rein, *Dilemmas of Welfare Policy: Why Work Strategies Haven't Worked* (New York: Praeger Publishers, 1982), 145.

13. Ibid., 55. See also Frank C. Pierson, *The Minimum Level of Employment and Public Policy* (Kalamazoo, Michigan: W.E. Upjohn Institute for Employment Research, 1980), 93. Rein felt that her research conclusions were affected by the welfare recipients' lack of understanding of the income disregard provisions, and the lack of adequate funding for child care, transportation, and other support services. Pierson felt the income disregard provision did not provide enough of an incentive to offset additional taxes and possible loss of some other benefits, i.e., Medicaid or child care.

14. Thomas Fraker, Robert Moffitt, and Douglas Wolf, "Effective Tax Rates and Guarantees in the AFDC Program, 1967–1982, *The Journal of Human Resources* 20 (1985): 252.

15. Robert Moffitt, "Work Incentives in the AFDC System: An Analysis of the 1981 Reforms," *The American Economic Review* 76 (May 1986): 219.

16. Ibid.

17. U.S. General Accounting Office, *CWEP's Implementation Results to Date Raise Questions About the Administration's Proposed Mandatory Workfare Program* (Washington, D.C.: U. S. General Accounting Office, 1984), 5.

18. Dickinson, "Which Welfare Strategies Work?," 267.

19. Kondratas, "The Political Economy of Work-for-Welfare," 229.

20. Ibid., 235, and Dickinson, "Which Welfare Strategies Work?," 268.

21. Rein, *Dilemmas of Welfare Policy*, 69.

22. Kondratas, "The Political Economy of Work-for Welfare," 239.

23. Philip Robins, "A Comparison of the Labor Supply Findings from Four Negative Income Tax Experiments," *The Journal of Human Resources* 20 (Fall 1985): 567.

24. Ibid., 568.

25. Ibid., 580.

26. Ibid.

27. Gary Burtless and Robert Haveman, "Policy Lessons from Three Labor Market Experiments," *Employment and Training R&D* (Kalamazoo, Michigan: W.E. Upjohn Institute for Employment Research, 1984), 109.

28. Ibid., 109–110.

29. Ibid., 110.

30. Ibid., 111.

31. Ibid., 112.

32. Ibid., 112.

33. Ibid., 113.

34. David M. Blau and Philip K. Robins, "Labor Supply Response to Welfare Programs: A Dynamic Analysis," *Journal of Labor Economics* 4 (January 1986): 83.

35. Ibid. Qualitative choice theory considers work disincentives to explain observed patterns of duration and frequency of occurrence of employment, unemployment, and nonparticipation spells over time ver-

sus static random utility qualitative choice models which have been traditionally used to analyze cross-sectional labor force data at a point in time, i.e., for one occurrence of an employment, unemployment, or nonparticipation spell.

36. Ibid., 101.
37. Ibid.
38. Ibid., 102.
39. National Governors Association, *INFOLETTER* (August 27, 1986).
40. Judith M. Gueron, *Work Incentives for Welfare Recipients: Lessons from a Multi-State Experiment* (New York: Manpower Demonstration Research Corporation, 1986), 733. See also Dickinson, "Which Welfare Strategies Work?," 267–268. The participation obligation of the WIN program was, in effect, only a registration obligation. The majority of WIN mandatory registrants were never required to participate in a WIN program component. Dickinson and others have criticized WIN for its inadequate funding level, which precluded both mandatory and voluntary registrants from having access to WIN-funded job-training or employment slots.
41. Dickinson, "Which Welfare Strategies Work?," 267, and U.S. General Accounting Office, *CWEP's Implementation Results to Date.*
42. Dickinson, "Which Welfare Strategies Work?," 267–268.
43. Ibid., 267.
44. Ibid.
45. Ibid., 267–268.
46. Manpower Demonstration Research Corporation, *Interim Findings from the Demonstration of State Work/Welfare Initiatives* (New York: MDRC, 1986), 14–15.
47. Gueron, *Work Incentives for Welfare Recipients,* 737–738, and MDRC, *Interim Findings from the Demonstration of State Work/Welfare Initiatives,* 14–15.
48. U.S. General Accounting Office, *CWEP's Implementation Results to Date,* and Dickinson, "Which Welfare Strategies Work?," 268–270.
49. Dickinson, "Which Welfare Strategies Work?," 268–70.
50. MDRC, *Interim Findings from the Demonstration of State Work/Welfare Initiatives,* 13–14, and Gueron, Work Incentives for Welfare Recipients, 735–736.
51. Judith M. Gueron, "Welfare to Work Programs: Lessons on

Recent State Initiatives," *Policy Studies Review* 6 (May 1987): 733–743.

52. Ibid.
53. Ibid.
54. Ibid.

III

Poverty and Public Assistance: The Theoretical Perspective

The proposed program, our final and most ambitious thought experiment, consists of scrapping the entire federal welfare and income-support structure for working-aged persons, including AFDC, Medicaid, Food Stamps, Unemployment Insurance, Workers' Compensation, subsidized housing, disability insurance, and the rest. It would leave the working-aged person with no recourse whatsoever except the job market, family members, friends, and public or private locally funded services. It is the Alexandrian solution: cut the knot, for there is no way to untie it.[1]

Given the resources devoted to fighting poverty, we have done about as well as we could have hoped. There is a logic to the broad outlines of the current "safety net." Using categorical programs, we have provided financial support to the needy and probably have not caused a very appreciable share of the current problems.[2]

Right and left now recognize that neither robust economic growth nor massive government transfer payments can by themselves transform a "community" where 90 percent of the children are born into fatherless families, where over 60 percent of the population

is on welfare, where the work ethic has evaporated and
the entrepreneurial drive is channeled into gangs and
drug-pushing.[3]

My reading of evidence on manpower programs
does not correspond to the widespread view in the press
that "nothing works" or "nothing works well." It would
be more accurate to say that "nothing works miracles."[4]

As the above opinions indicate, considerable controversy exists
concerning the propriety and effectiveness of past and present public
welfare policy in this country. Normative issues continue to be debated,
such as the role of the federal government in addressing poverty and the
appropriateness of the various mechanisms used to translate policy goals
into outcomes. For instance, noted scholars such as Charles Murray and
Lawrence Mead claim our national poverty policy and the resulting income maintenance system inhibit labor force attachment and cause individuals to voluntarily reduce their work effort. They believe our system
of social welfare has created a population segment dependent on public
assistance as an alternative to labor market participation.

Many of the unresolved issues concerning policy goals and anti-
poverty strategies are grounded in competing ideological paradigms and
theoretical perspectives which tend to complicate inquiry into the issues
regarding poverty and welfare dependency. While it is possible that the
ideological nature of the problem may preclude a true policy consensus
on the best method to reduce poverty, questions relative to specific program efficiency, effectiveness of various intervention strategies, and program goal attainment do lend themselves to empirical analysis.

Prior to examining the analytical phase of this study, it will be
beneficial to first review the major theoretical explanations for poverty,
public assistance, and anti-poverty programs and the relationships between poverty and public assistance.

POVERTY AND PUBLIC ASSISTANCE

In the United States, only the poor receive public assistance in the
form of Aid to Families with Dependent Children (AFDC). In order to
receive AFDC, families must pass a "means" test, that is, they must prove
they lack the resources necessary to sustain daily life. AFDC, however,

is not intended to move a poor family above the poverty line. In all fifty states, the income threshold for receiving AFDC is below the officially established poverty level. For instance, in 1988 only sixteen states paid AFDC benefits that were above 80 percent of the poverty level for a family of three, the average size of a family receiving AFDC. Eight states paid benefits that were less than 60 percent of the poverty level.[5] In Missouri, the maximum AFDC grant amount for a family of three is $292. This amount is only 30 percent of the official poverty level indicated on table 3-1.[6]

Poverty is most often defined in one of two ways, in either absolute or relative terms. An absolute definition of poverty defines an income amount necessary to achieve a minimal level of well-being. This minimum level changes with fluctuations in the general standard of living and with the value of money. Though always tied to the cost of certain kinds of material goods, this minimum income level also implies psychic consequences for those living below its standard. Feelings of helplessness and powerlessness in the face of overwhelming political, economic, and social forces help keep such persons mired in poverty.[7]

TABLE 3-1

U.S. DEPARTMENT OF HEALTH AND HUMAN SERVICES
SOCIAL SECURITY ADMINISTRATION, 1992 POVERTY LEVEL GUIDELINES

SIZE OF FAMILY UNIT	POVERTY GUIDELINE	
	Annual	Monthly
1	$ 6,810	$ 568
2	9,190	766
3	11,570	964
4	13,950	1,162
5	16,330	1,360
6	18,710	1,559
7	21,090	1,758
8	23,470	1,956

NOTE: For family units with more than eight members, add $2,380 annually for each additional member. Monthly data are rounded.
SOURCE: February 14, 1992, *Federal Register* (Vol. 57, No. 31, p. 5455).

Relative definitions do not relate poverty to particular level of material well-being but to the well-being of other members of society. For instance, in a relative definition of poverty, a family is poor if its resources place it well below a normal standard of living, no matter how moderate or extravagant that standard might be. Most relative definitions of poverty define poverty as any family income below one-half the nation's median family income. It is evident that the type of definition chosen and the mechanics of the poverty calculation make a big difference in evaluating policy. Under most absolute definitions, poverty has varied in the last thirty years. Employing relative definitions, however, the proportion of poor in America has remained relatively constant during these years.[8]

Table 3-2 compares the poverty rates for selected years using the official poverty measure and the alternative relative measure at 50 percent of median income.[9]

TABLE 3-2

POVERTY RATES FOR SELECTED YEARS UNDER THE
OFFICIAL MEASURE AND RELATIVE MEASURE

YEAR	OFFICIAL MEASURE	RELATIVE MEASURE AT 50% OF MEDIAN INCOME
1972	11.9 %	17.9%
1977	11.6	17.4
1982	15.0	18.9
1987	13.5	19.7
1988	13.0	19.5

SOURCE: Calculated from the Current Population Survey for years shown. Patricia Ruggles, "Measuring Poverty," *Focus,* Vol. 14, No. 1 (Spring 1992).

The official and most commonly used measurement to identify who and how many people live in poverty is the one established by the Social Security Administration in the 1960s. This poverty measurement is revised yearly to account for changes in the cost of living variables used in the poverty formula. As table 3-3 indicates, there has been considerable change in the official poverty rate since one was first calculated for 1959.

TABLE 3-3[10]

POVERTY RATES FOR SELECTED YEARS 1959–1990

YEAR	U.S. POVERTY RATE	MISSOURI POVERTY RATE
1959	22.4%	24.9%
1964	19.0	NA
1969	12.1	14.7
1974	11.2	NA
1979	11.7	11.8
1984	14.4	14.5
1989	12.8	12.6
1990	13.5	13.4

SOURCE: U.S. Department of Commerce, *Current Population Reports*, Consumer Income Series P-60 (August 1991).

As would be expected, the official poverty rate has come under criticism in recent years as unrealistic by today's standards. The official U.S. poverty standard evolved further from a series of studies undertaken by Mollie Orshansky for the Social Security Administration in 1963. Ms. Orshansky's poverty formula was based on data from the Department of Agriculture identifying a "minimally" adequate food budget which was than multiplied by a factor of three, on the assumption that food typically represents about one-third of the total family expenditures. The one-third estimate was derived from a 1955 food consumption survey, and was probably already outdated in 1963 when first used, since consumption data from 1960–61 indicate that food consumption was closer to one-fourth the typical budget by then.[11]

Basically, any family whose income was less than three times the cost of the minimum food budget of the Department of Agriculture was classified as poor. The original Orshansky measure has been updated for changes in prices since the 1960s, but it has not been updated to account for changes in needs or consumption patterns that have occurred over time. Beyond this, income for the purpose of measuring poverty, consists of money income before taxes and does not include non-cash forms of income such as food stamps or Medicaid; however, cash income from government transfer payments are included in the calculation.[12]

In addition to complaints that the calculation multiplier is artificially low, critics of the government's official poverty measure also point out that the food budget central to the calculation is too low, for example, allowing about $2.75 per person per day for food in 1989. Also, the formula does not take into account regional differences in the cost of living, and it is adjusted to increases in the consumer price index rather than the actual cost of food which is the key variable in this formula.

One interesting point about the poverty formula is that pre-tax cash income, including government transfer payments, social insurance and AFDC payments, are counted as cash income. If the definition of poverty were changed to exclude government transfer payments, nearly 25 percent of the population would be poor, even using the seemingly low Social Security Administration definition. On the other hand, if the official poverty figures took into account the income value of in-kind benefits such as food stamps, medical care or housing assistance in addition to people's tendency to under-report income, these factors would lower the poverty rate to approximately 8 percent.[13]

As noted above, all fifty states have AFDC benefits lower than the official poverty threshold. Each state sets its own standard of need for food, clothing, and shelter, and then AFDC payments are calculated on this formula. Families with countable incomes below the standard are eligible for aid; however, states are not required to pay benefits at 100 percent of the standard of need and few states do so. The state standard-of-need formulas do not attempt to move people above the poverty line. For example, in 1987 the median standard of need for all states for a family of three was $428 a month while the states' median AFDC benefit was only $354 per month for a family of three. In 1987, AFDC benefits for a family of three ranged from a high of $533 per month in California to a low of $114 in Alabama.[14]

Presently in Missouri, the standard of need for a family of three is

$312 while the maximum AFDC grant for the family is $292. If the maximum food stamp grant were also counted, this family would receive a total of $584 per month. This same family would need $964 to rise above the poverty line.[15]

The above discussion points out the problems with the current definition of poverty and the level of AFDC support provided to families. It leads one to question whether our present system of income maintenance is providing an adequate level of support to our country's poor. It also points out the problems caused by competing policy goals: on the one hand, to provide a basic level of support for the poor, while on the other hand, not to provide support so generous that it encourages people to avoid work and become dependent on government public assistance payments. As Adam Smith put it more than two hundred years ago, poverty is a lack of those necessities that "the custom of the country renders it indecent for creditable people, even of the lowest order, to be without."[16] When analyzing poverty statistics, however, one should keep in mind that the typical family of three AFDC recipients is a single mother and two children. The two children represent two-thirds of all the people receiving AFDC in the nation. Many would argue that children should be guaranteed an adequate level of support without being expected to work or assume responsibility for the actions of their parents.

COMPETING PARADIGMS

There are several theoretical perspectives which offer explanations for poverty, anti-poverty, and public assistance programs. For the purpose of comparison, however, Clarke Cochrane's conservative-liberal theory dichotomy consolidates the major tenets of the various theories into two competing paradigms, pro-welfare and anti-welfare. While Cochrane's dichotomy is a less-than-perfect description of the theoretical perspectives relative to issues of poverty, public assistance dependency, income redistribution policy, welfare reform, and the proper role of government as it relates to these issues, it does provide a broad framework for classification of the general tenets of each position. It must be understood, however, that there can be considerable overlap on any specific issue between the two factions.

According to Clarke Cochrane in *The Double Bind: Income Support or Welfare Dependence*, "As much as they disagree about the definition and incidence of poverty, ideological groups disagree even more about its causes."[17] Cochrane states scholars such as Charles Murray and Robert Rector posit that poverty is not a problem in the United States since most poverty is voluntary. The free enterprise system in the United States offers opportunities and a decent standard of living to anyone who is willing to work. Individuals who cannot work because of their age, handicap, or disability have access to the government's social insurance system or to private philanthropic organizations. Anti-welfare theorists argue that healthy adults who are poor lack the self-discipline to work hard and delay immediate pleasure in the interest of gaining a better future. They believe the poor choose not to take advantage of educational and employment opportunities that are available to everyone.

Cochrane believes the anti-welfare camp is quick to adopt the "culture of poverty" premise which holds that the attitudes of the poor are different from those of the working classes. This position holds that the poor learn these attitudes from their culture which teaches them satisfaction with a life of casual social relationships, irresponsibility, immediate gratification, and sexual license. In addition, they argue that government welfare and anti-poverty programs will not have an impact on poverty since they do not attempt to change the basic attitudes of the poor. They perceive government programs provide such a generous standard of living to the poor that they are encouraged to remain on the government programs, not work, and stay in poverty.

According to Cochrane, welfare opponents believe government programs encourage families to break up and reward sexual license by increasing welfare benefits for additional and often illegitimate children, while making little demand for behavioral changes. In effect, government social programs make it too attractive for people not to work. Moreover, they feel that the growth of government and the resulting increase of regulation and interference in the private sector has weakened the productive capacity of business. Government programs and regulations, such as Aid to Families with Dependent Children and the minimum wage laws, actually result in reduced opportunities for the people who need the opportunities the most. Because of these programs, the poor have a viable alternative to work and employers are discouraged from providing job experience to people who need it because of the high labor costs.

Cochrane believes that welfare opponents also tend to be skeptical of anti-poverty employment and training programs such as the present Job Opportunities and Basic Skills Training Program. They view this and similar programs as a disguised form of welfare or as government make-work programs. While believing in mandatory work or work training in order to receive welfare, opponents feel that the private sector is in the best position to train and employ the able-bodied welfare recipient. They believe the government should encourage the private sector to increase production and employment through deregulation of industry, tax cuts, and tax credits and incentives for businesses that hire the jobless.

Conversely, theorists such as Senator Daniel Patrick Moynihan, Sara McLanahan, and Sar Levithan tend to view the problem of poverty quite differently. They espouse the view that a genuine lack of opportunities for the poor is the central cause of poverty. They argue that the poor are no different from the non-poor except that they do not have the same opportunities to obtain an education, job training, employment, or decent and affordable housing. They believe that the poor would take advantage of genuine opportunities to increase their education and job skills if these opportunities actually existed.

According to Cochrane, the pro-welfare camp also assess the impact of government income maintenance and anti-poverty programs differently from the anti-welfare perspective. For instance, they reject allegations that the AFDC program is responsible for the demise of the work ethic in the United States. They argue that there is no firm evidence that AFDC in itself leads to dependency, encourages family dissolution, or increased illegitimacy. In fact, welfare proponents argue that AFDC is doing what it was intended to do—which is to provide temporary assistance to needy families during a time of economic crises. To support this contention they point out that research continues to demonstrate that the average AFDC family receives AFDC for less than two years. They also note that several studies have found that the typical income of AFDC families over a period of time often contains as much income from labor market earnings as from AFDC.[18]

To reduce the incidence of poverty, Cochrane feels proponents advocate more social programs that provide real opportunities to obtain education, skills, or jobs. "They emphasize that the opportunities offered to the poor must be real. The poor rightly refuse to exploit job-training programs that do not provide salable skills or that provide employment only in temporary, menial work with no future."[19]

With regard to the "culture of poverty" theory, Cochrane feels the pro-welfare camp tends to recognize that the culture of poverty exists but offers an alternative explanation for its existence. Welfare proponents view the culture of poverty as resulting from of a realistic assessment by the poor of their chances of escaping poverty in a society and economy that is structured against them. Proponents posit that discrimination against racial minorities and women, especially single mothers who head families, is a primary cause of poverty. They believe that discrimination continues to be pervasive in our society, has a detrimental effect on the education, job opportunities, advancement opportunities, and wages of the groups discriminated against. In other words, Cochrane feels welfare advocates view the culture of poverty as an expression of the hopelessness felt by the people living in poverty who see no way out.

In opposition to the anti-welfare perspective, Cochrane states that proponents tend to view the capitalistic system as contributing to the cause of the poverty problem, and not the solution to the problem. They see poverty as one of the harmful side effects of our capitalistic system. Economic progress inherent in the capitalistic system causes some job skills to become obsolete resulting in unemployment, reduced wages, and increased poverty.

In their view of capitalism contributing to poverty, welfare proponents are joined by more-radical theorists such as Karl Marx who wrote more than one hundred years ago. These more-radical economic theorists view poverty as a central component and a necessary feature of capitalism. They see poverty as a functional feature of capitalism since it creates a pool of surplus laborers who tend to keep wages lower and who are available to take the low-wage, menial, dirty jobs that the middle class does not want. Poverty also helps keep the middle class in its place by providing an example of the consequences arising from a deterioration of the work ethic.

Cochrane feels welfare reform advocates generally believe that government policy in regard to anti-poverty programs should place an emphasis on increased education and employment opportunities as opposed to the conservative solution of mandatory work requirements and incentives for private business. Reform advocates tend to place more emphasis on increasing the human capital of the poor by improving their level of education and job skills, and they hold that mandatory work programs without remedial education and support services such as child care do little to move people off welfare and out of poverty.

The radicals, according to Cochrane, take this position several steps further, arguing that the present system of public assistance and anti-poverty programs do little more than institutionalize poverty and temporarily pacify workers. They posit that poverty will not be eliminated until government takes control of the private sector, halting technological changes which eliminate jobs and giving workers an active role in the decision-making process.

MODELS OF DEPENDENCY

In a recent review of interdisciplinary literature concerning poverty and welfare, David T. Ellwood of Harvard University moves the discussion of poverty from the theoretical pro-welfare/anti-welfare dichotomy examined above to specific models or theories of dependency. Ellwood notes that recent literature contains a shift away from economic explanations for poverty, such as labor supply response, tax rates, and opportunity, toward behavioral dependency explanations. According to Ellwood:

> The transformation of the debate is extraordinary, for a focus on dependency represents more than a change in terms. It represents an implicit shift in behavioral models. In earlier debates, economists seemed to dominate, with their emphasis on static choice models: behavior could be understood by examining the choices people face at any point in time, and changes in behavior could be made by altering the available choices. Now the talk is often about lost confidence or distorted values that leave the poor with little desire to take control of their lives.[20]

Ellwood's review of the recent literature identified several models that attempted to explain behavioral dependency. The three types of models that seemed particularly helpful in attempting to interpret dependency were the expectancy models, cultural models, and rational choice models. Each emphasizes different factors and a different conception of behavior, respectively emphasizing confidence and control, values and culture, and choices and incentives. When interpreting these models, Ellwood emphasizes that "the reader needs to realize that the models suggest that a preoccupation with attitudes and behavior of the dependent is myopic, and that judgments about values cannot be made without understanding larger social issues."[21]

The first of Ellwood's three categories of models is expectancy models. Expectancy theory presupposes a reciprocal relationship between confidence and a sense of control on the one hand and what actually happens to people on the other. In other words, those who succeed gain confidence while those who fail lose confidence. People who repetitively fail will lose their motivation to try; they will fear failure so much that they will stop trying to succeed.[22]

According to expectancy theorists, welfare dependency results when people lose a sense of control over their lives and cease to believe that they can realistically become self-sufficient. People become overwhelmed by circumstances and lose the capacity to use available opportunities to change their condition. Generally, expectancy models call for consideration of more than just current choices since past successes and failures as well as current perceptions are all critical components of a model that emphasizes confidence and control.

Expectancy models suggest that the variables linked to control and confidence will influence dependency. They imply that for some individuals, welfare becomes a trap that increases the individual's passivity and isolation. In addition, the increased isolation and feelings of lack of control decrease feelings of self-worth which in turn play a critical role in family structure patterns.

The second of the three categories of models identified by Ellwood is cultural models. Cultural models typically emphasize that groups within society have different values, orientations, and expectations. According to Ellwood, the most extreme example of cultural models is the culture-of-poverty hypothesis. Culture-of-poverty characterizations, such as Kenneth Auletta's underclass, envision a population that "feels excluded from society, rejects commonly accepted values, and suffers from behavioral as well as income deficiencies. They don't just tend to be poor; to most Americans their behavior seems aberrant."[23]

To some extent, most theories on welfare dependency include the notion that culture or norms influence behavior to some extent. The cultural literature on dependency, however, claims that the values, attitudes, and expectations of the underclass sub-group are well outside those of the mainstream. For such adverse values to develop and persist, groups of people must be isolated geographically and socially from the rest of society. These people live in geographic areas of concentrated deprivation, where an underclass can be maintained.[24]

As discussed earlier, both liberals and conservatives recognize the culture of poverty but offer different explanations for its existence. Also, while both sides have identified common features of the cultural model as being critical, such as geographic concentration and isolation, they tend to emphasize different explanations for the resulting dependency. For instance, liberals view the geographic concentrations as a result of the loss of jobs and restraints on mobility of poor minority residents. Conservatives see welfare and government benefits as the problem since they offer a culturally or socially acceptable alternative to working.

Besides geographic concentration, the cultural model views intergenerational transfer of cultural traits as a serious consequence. "Families with distorted values, or children raised in homes where welfare was the primary source of income, find welfare, out-of-wedlock births, and lack of work a normal and acceptable fact of life."[25] As a result the pathologies of one generation are passed on to the next.

In cultural models, values are viewed as the major problem. Groups of disadvantaged and relatively unsuccessful people who share the same values often pass their values to succeeding generations. These groups live together, having little contact with the rest of society.

The third of Ellwood's three categories of models is choice models, which Ellwood considers the dominant paradigm in both economics and policy analysis. According to choice or rational choice models, long-term welfare dependence is seen as a series of reasoned choices in light of available options. The attributes of both the welfare system and the nature of outside opportunities are seen to influence choice. Rational choice models assume that individuals examine the options they face, evaluate them according to their preferences and then select the option that presents the greatest utility or satisfaction. In addition, choice models require the understanding of both available choices and the preferences of the person choosing.

When evaluating choice models of welfare dependency, it is necessary to distinguish between bad choices and bad preferences. Choice models, when applied to the issue of welfare dependency, often indicate that the rational choice for a typical single welfare mother with two children, is to remain on welfare rather than take the typical minimum-wage job with no health benefits. In many states, a woman is economically better off receiving welfare, at least in the short term. If a single mother leaves welfare to work in a minimum-wage job, she will often see no increase in her disposable income. In fact, in some states with high welfare grants, her financial condition may worsen.

As Ellwood points out:

One of the more interesting and striking results of
the choice model is that, absent opportunities to leave
welfare through marriage or other nonemployment
routes, people ought to stay on welfare a long time.
The model suggests that it is hard to earn one's way off
welfare. Thus it predicts that earnings exits would be
rare, and they ought to be particularly rare for those
with low earnings potential, high work expenses, or high
welfare benefits.[26]

Ellwood and others who have studied the welfare dependency issue realize that no one theory provides the key insights that will tell
policymakers how to resolve the welfare problem. Research indicates that
regardless of the paradigm utilized, moderate policy changes will not make
a large difference in welfare use and produce only limited changes in
behavior:

Employment and training programs have had only
modest results, and as long as programs look roughly
like they do now, there is little evidence that the welfare roles will increase or decrease even if the most
liberal or conservative welfare reform plans are adopted,
other than eliminating welfare altogether.[27]

THE ECONOMICS OF PUBLIC ASSISTANCE

As the above theories of dependency indicate, families become
dependent on welfare for various reasons. However, regardless of ideological orientation or belief in a dominant welfare-dependency paradigm,
the fact remains that welfare and other government benefits do provide
an alternative to work. As long as welfare is an alternative to work, clearly
the willingness of individuals to work is affected by the relationship between their earnings potential and the level of their welfare benefits.

Moreover, the majority of all AFDC recipients live in families
headed by single mothers who are either divorced, separated, or never
married. Numerous studies indicate that female-headed families face a
much higher risk of poverty than any other demographic group. According to the official government definition of poverty, roughly one out of
every two single mothers is poor. Many others who escape living in the

legal definition of poverty still live barely above impoverishment. Duncan and Hoffman found that one year after divorce, the average income of the most fortunate half of single mothers is equal to only 60 percent of their pre-divorce income.[28]

The major source of income for all families, except those headed by widows, is the earnings of the family head. Therefore, the ability of a single mother to earn income is critical to her family's economic status; however, female family heads earn only about one-third as much as married fathers, partly because they work fewer hours and partly because they have lower earnings. For instance, Garfinkel and McLanahan found that in 1982, the average earned income of a family head in a white married family was $21,932. In families headed by a white mother, comparable earnings were $7,666. In black families, the earnings of the family head were $13,508 in two-parent families and $5,363 in mother-only families.[29] In addition, Garfinkel and McLanahan note that these data reflect a selection process that channels women with higher earnings capacity into the labor force and women with lower earnings capacity into home-maker and welfare status.

It is apparent that there is good reason to believe that for a large number of women receiving welfare, working will not immediately improve their economic situation and allow them to earn their way out of poverty. In many instances, even if a woman worked full time for a full year in a minimum-wage job, she would not have any more disposable income than a nonworking woman who receives welfare. For instance, table 3-4 indicates the disposable income of a typical mother and two children, by earnings.

As table 3-4 indicates, a woman who earns ten thousand dollars a year (or roughly five dollars an hour) in Pennsylvania, is only slightly better off than one who does not work at all. Her disposable income will have risen only about fifteen hundred dollars while she will have lost her Medicaid protection. Her five-dollar-an-hour job may not include health benefits to replace Medicaid. Even if she finds a job paying fifteen thousand dollars per year (seven dollars and fifty cents per hour), her disposable income will be only about twenty-five hundred dollars higher than that of a woman who does not work and collects welfare.[31]

Presently in Missouri, which has one of the lowest AFDC grants in the nation, the combined maximum AFDC and food stamp benefit for a family of three is $584 per month, or $7,008 per year. This family will also receive Medicaid, and may receive housing assistance, energy assis-

TABLE 3-4[30]

EARNINGS AND BENEFITS FOR A SINGLE MOTHER WITH TWO CHILDREN WITH DAY CARE EXPENSES, AFTER FOUR MONTHS ON JOB

JANUARY 1989, PENNSYLVANIA

EARNINGS	EITC	AFDC[c]	FOOD STAMPS	MEDICAID	SOCIAL SECURITY TAX	FEDERAL INCOME TAX	STATE INCOME TAX	WORK EXPENSES[d]	"DISPOSABLE" INCOME
0	0	$4,824	$1,766	Yes	0	0	0	0	$6,590[e]
$2,000	$280	4,204	1,525	Yes	$150	0	0	$600	7,259[e]
4,000	560	2,324	1,662	Yes	300	0	0	1,200	7,046[e]
5,000	700	1,384	1,730	Yes	376	0	0	1,500	6,938[e]
6,000	840	444	1,799	Yes	451	0	0	1,800	6,832[e]
7,000	910	0	1,735	Yes	526	0	0	2,100	7,019[e]
8,000	910	0	1,555	Yes[f]	601	0	$168	2,400	7,296[e]
9,000	910	0	1,375	Yes[f]	676	0	189	2,700	7,720[e]
10,000	910	0	1,195	No[g]	751	0	210	3,000	8,144
15,000	434	0	0	No	1,127	$668	315	4,200	9,124
20,000	0	0	0	No	1,502	1,418	420	5,040	11,620
30,000	0	0	0	No	2,253	2,918	630	5,040	19,159
50,000	0	0	0	No	3,605	7,816	1,050	5,040	32,489

SOURCE: Committee on Ways and Means, U.S. House of Representatives, Background Material and Data on Programs within the Jurisdiction of the Committee on Ways and Means (Washington, D.C.: U.S. Government Printing Office, 1989), pp. 536–537.

NOTE: Under IRS rules, unless earnings at least equal Aid to Families with Dependent Children, the mother generally is not a "head of household" eligible for EITC (Earned Income Tax Credit); but it appears that this rule is rarely applied. Example assumes rule is not applied.

[a] Assumes these deductions: $105 monthly standard allowance (would drop to $75 after one year on job) and child care costs equal to 20 percent of earnings, up to max. of $320 for two children.

[b] Assumes these deductions: 20 percent of earnings (including EITC as earnings), $102 monthly standard deduction and child care costs equal to 20 percent of wages, up to maximum of $320 for two children.

[c] Head-of-household rates in effect for 1989.

[d] Assumed to equal 10 percent of earnings up to maximum of $100 monthly, plus child care costs equal to 20 percent of earnings up to the maximum allowed by AFDC, and food stamps ($320 for two children).

[e] In addition, the benefits from Medicaid could be added, but are not. Medicaid in fiscal year 1986 cost about $1,994 for a three-person AFDC family (national average). In Pennsylvania, the cost of Medicaid for a three-person family in fiscal year 1986 was $1,775.

[f] Family would qualify for Medicaid for nine additional months under 1984 federal law, which requires state to continue Medicaid that long for a family whose earnings removed them from AFDC, provided the family would have retained AFDC eligibility if $30 monthly and one-third of residual earnings had been disregarded beyond four months.

[g] To regain Medicaid eligibility, family must spend down on medical expenses to state's medically needy limit ($5,100, as of July 1987).

SOURCE: Institute for Research on Poverty, *Focus*, Vol. 12, No.1 (Spring 1989), p. 8.

tance, child-care assistance, and possibly education assistance. Moreover, the AFDC recipient does not have work expenses or taxes. In addition, this person will have considerable leisure time in comparison to single mother who works forty hours a week. In contrast, a single mother with two children who works two thousand hours a year at five dollars an hour will earn $833 a month or ten thousand dollars a year. She will pay taxes, have work-related expenses, possibly have child-care expenses, and may not receive health-care benefits from her employer.

It is obvious that for some individuals, welfare does provide an alternative to working. The welfare alternative is most attractive when the single mother is unable to work full time, her education and lack of job skills limit her to low-paying, dead-end jobs, her work expenses including child care are high, her job does not include health benefits, and state welfare benefits are high. Under these conditions, work may make little financial sense.

Overall, AFDC assistance is generally acknowledged to be beneficial to many impoverished persons, particularly since it keeps children from starving. Yet, AFDC is like a prescription drug with side effects. For AFDC recipients these side effects include lowered self-esteem, impairment in gaining economic benefits from low-paying jobs, and increased dependency on assistance from the government.

NOTES

1. Charles Murray, *Losing Ground: American Social Policy,* 1950–1980 (New York: Basic Books, 1984), 227–228.

2. David Ellwood and Lawrence Summers, "Poverty in America: Is Welfare the Answer or the Problem?" U.S. Department of Health and Human Services Conference on Poverty and Policy, Williamsburg, Virginia (December 1984), 13.

3. Mickey Kaus, "The Work Ethic State," *The New Republic* (July 1986), 2–33.

4. Gary Burtless, "Public Spending for the Poor: The Last Twenty Years," *Focus* 8 (Spring 1985): 13.

5. Clarke E. Cochrane et al., "The Double Bind: Income Support or Welfare Dependence," *American Public Policy*, 3rd Edition, (New York: St. Martin's Press, 1990), 228.

6. U.S. Department of Health and Human Services, *Federal Register* 57 (February 14, 1992): 5455.

7. Clarke E. Cochrane, "The Double Bind: Income Support or Welfare Dependence," 212.

8. Ibid.

9. Patricia Ruggles, "Measuring Poverty," *Focus* 14 (Spring 1992): 7.

10. U.S. Department of Commerce, *Current Population Reports*, Consumer Income Series P-60, No. 175 (August 1991): 16 and 219–221.

11. Patricia Ruggles, "Measuring Poverty," 2.

12. Ibid., 3.

13. Clarke E. Cochrane, "The Double Bind: Income Support or Welfare Dependence," 217.

14. Ibid., 228.

15. Greg Vadner, Deputy Director for Income Maintenance, Missouri Department of Social Services, Division of Family Services, interview with author, 17 June 1992.

16. Patricia Ruggles, "Measuring Poverty," 1.

17. Clarke E. Cochrane, "The Double Bind: Income Support or Welfare Dependence," 220. For the general tenants of the conservative, liberal, and radical positions see Charles Murray, *Losing Ground: American Social Policy 1950–1980* (New York: Basic Books, 1984); Robert Rector, *The Paradox of Poverty: How We Spent $3.5 Trillion Without Changing the Poverty Rate* (The Heritage Foundation, No. 410, Wash-

ington, D.C., 1992); William Julius Wilson, *The Truly Disadvantaged: The Inner City, The Underclass, and Public Policy* (Chicago: University of Chicago Press, 1987); Sara McLanahan and others, "Family Structure, Poverty, and the Underclass," Institute for Research on Poverty, Discussion Paper No. 823-87 (University of Wisconsin-Madison, March 1987); Sar A. Levithan, *Programs in Aid of the Poor* (Baltimore: The Johns Hopkins University Press, 1985); Richard Quinney, *Class, State, and Crime* (New York: McKay, 1977), 25, for a discussion of Marxism and its focus on the oppression of capitalist society; Herbert Marcuse, *Socialist Humanism*, edited by Erich Fromm, (New York: Doubleday, 1965). Also see, for a discussion of the various theories, Chaim I. Waxman, *The Stigma of Poverty* (Elmsford, N.Y.: Pergamon, 1983).

18. Greg J. Duncan and Saul D. Hoffman, "The Use and Effects of Welfare: A Survey of Recent Evidence," 3. Paper presented at the conference on The Political Economy of the Transfer Society, Tallahassee, Florida, November 1987.

19. Clarke E. Cochrane, "The Double Bind: Income Support or Welfare Dependence," 221.

20. David T. Ellwood, "The Origins of 'Dependency': Choices, Confidence, or Culture?" *Focus* 12 (Spring/Summer 1989): 6.

21. Ibid.

22. Ibid., 9–10.

23. Ibid., 10–11. See also Kenneth Auletta, *The Underclass* (New York: Random House, 1982).

24. Ellwood, "The Origins of 'Dependency': Choices, Confidence, or Culture?" 10–11.

25. Ibid., 11.

26. Ibid., 6–9.

27. Ibid., 12.

28. Irwin Garfinkel, "Welfare Policy In America," Institute for Research on Poverty, University of Wisconsin-Madison, Discussion Paper No. 847-87 (October 1987): 7.

29. Ibid., 9.

30. David T. Ellwood, 8.

31. Ibid.

IV

The Family Support Act of 1988, Job Opportunities and Basic Skills Training Program (JOBS)

> Welfare was never meant to be a lifestyle; it was never meant to be a habit; it was never supposed to be passed from generation to generation like a legacy. It's time to replace the assumptions of the welfare state and help reform the welfare system.[1]

Since its inception in the 1930s, public assistance or "welfare" in the form of Aid to Families with Dependent Children (AFDC) has been an unpopular, and often divisive, program. As discussed in chapter 3, some theorists attribute poverty to the failings of the economy or the educational system, or to structural barriers inherent in our social systems. Others see poverty as the result of deficient values and moral failings of the poor. Disagreements over the causes of poverty have fueled arguments about the programs that government should and should not undertake to reduce poverty, about the relative roles of the federal and state governments in implementing antipoverty policies, and about the responsibilities of welfare recipients.

In spite of these ideological disagreements, however, a surprising consensus between conservatives, moderates, and liberals began to develop in the late 1980s concerning the goals and priorities of new welfare reform legislation. Conservatives realized that labor market shortages and the growing need for a competitive workforce meant that any welfare program had to offer basic skills and job training. At the other extreme, liberals were willing to accept mandatory participation requirements and punitive sanctions for nonparticipation if programs provided education, training, and support services and were not merely "punitive work programs." This consensus resulted in the Family Support Act of 1988, Public Law 100-485.

THE NEW CONSENSUS

In his paper for *The Brookings Review*, "Welfare Reform: Will Consensus Be Enough," Robert D. Reischauer noted that:

> Liberals, moderates, and conservatives generally agreed about what is wrong with the current welfare system and what general directions reform should take. This consensus created, for the first time in decades, a relatively hospitable environment in which to formulate welfare policy, which, in turn, has allowed Congress to move forward with reform legislation.[2]

According to Reischauer, the new consensus involved five broad themes: the concepts of responsibility, work, family, education, and state discretion.

As Reischauer noted, discussion of these concepts in the context of welfare reform policy a decade earlier would have raised the hackles of both liberals and conservatives. Today these concepts are being proclaimed as a reaffirmation of basic "American values." Their widespread acceptance reflects changes in the political and economic environment as well as research findings of the Manpower Demonstration Research Corporation, and David Ellwood and Mary Jo Bane of Harvard University.[3]

The first concept central to welfare reform is responsibility, that is, the notion that public assistance should involve reciprocal responsibilities. This concept does not focus on the traditional entitlement aspect of welfare but instead emphasizes the concept of mutual obligation in which society's obligation to help the poor is balanced by the recipients' obligation to society. As a condition for receiving public assistance, recipients of assistance should fulfill their family responsibilities and strive to become self-sufficient. In return, society should provide adequate income and offer support services, training, and employment opportunities to help recipients meet their obligations.[4]

The second component of critical importance to any welfare reform consensus is the importance of work. Providing work for people who receive public assistance is more than just a strategy to reduce welfare costs and promote self-sufficiency. Work confers both emotional and psychological benefits on the recipient since work provides the opportunity to join the nation's mainstream. According to Reischauer, several reports, such as those issued by the National Governors Association, the American Public Welfare Association, and *A New Social Contract: Report of the New York Task Force on Poverty and Welfare* from the State of New York-Cuomo Commission, portray work as important to the development of personal dignity, self-confidence, and identity; plus, it is favorable to family stability and a healthy home environment. All of these reports recommended that able-bodied adult welfare recipients be obliged to prepare themselves for jobs, to look for work, and to accept employment when it is offered. In fact, the Cuomo report suggests that cash assistance be limited; moreover, it recommends that welfare recipients should be required to accept a publicly provided job within a certain time period or lose their welfare benefits.[5]

Next, the new consensus stresses the need to strengthen the family by making men responsible for their children and by reforming welfare regulations. Research indicates that a disproportionate number of poor live in families headed by females. Three out of every four new welfare cases result from either a marital disruption or birth to an unmarried woman. Over 40 percent of those who have a child under three when they first receive welfare remain on welfare for nine years or more.[6] Financial support from a child's father could help to alleviate the need for welfare in many situations. An additional problem is that state public assistance regulations contribute to family instability. Prior to 1988, twenty-four states restricted AFDC and Medicaid benefits to single-parent families, and many of the twenty-six states that offered benefits to two-parent families severely restricted eligibility so that only a small fraction of all poor, intact families received assistance.[7]

Another common theme of the new consensus is the need to emphasize education. High-school dropouts and people with low academic achievement are more likely to bear a child out of wedlock or to enter an unworkable marriage than are high school graduates with average achievement levels. Many poorly educated single mothers have little choice but to turn to the welfare system since they do not possess the basic skills employers demand for entry-level positions.

The new consensus recognizes that if poverty intervention strategies are to have long-term impacts on an individual's ability to remain employed, more attention has to be focused on education. Finally, the new consensus accepts the need to allow states more discretion and flexibility over certain aspects of welfare policy. In the past, the issue of state discretion sharply divided liberals and conservatives since liberals distrusted the states—particularly the southern states—which they felt showed little interest in either providing adequate benefits or in offering assistance in a nondiscriminatory fashion. Liberals favored the complete assumption of cash assistance by the federal government and the establishment of a national minimum benefit standard. Under the Reagan administration, however, the federal government became the primary force pushing for retrenchment of welfare programs. In fact, some traditionally conservative states emerged with important social policy innovations. For example, South Carolina has led in the area of indigent health care, and Arkansas and Tennessee in the area of education reform. In addition, the southern states improved their ability to administer welfare in a fair and professional manner, and the perception that states were not using their new discretion to run work-welfare demonstration projects in a punitive manner eased the fears of many liberals, which in turn led to a new consensus on welfare reform.[8]

THE FAMILY SUPPORT ACT

On October 13, 1988, President Reagan signed the Family Support Act of 1988, Public Law 100-485. The Family Support Act is widely viewed as the most significant development in welfare policy since the enactment of the Social Security Act of 1935, which established the Aid to Dependent Children program. The main change in welfare policy is in the direction of employment and training programs. The Family Support Act broke with traditional anti-poverty approaches by requiring that able-bodied welfare recipients pursue job training, education, or job-search assistance offered through Title II of the legislation entitled the Job Opportunities and Basic Skills Training Program (JOBS). Overall, the Family Support Act represents the most comprehensive approach for reducing welfare dependency and the most important change in the history of U.S. welfare policy. The Family Support Act addresses all five themes of what Reischauer termed the "new consensus" on welfare reform. The stated purpose of the Family Support Act is:

> To revise the AFDC program to emphasize work, child support, and family benefits, to amend title IV of the Social Security Act to encourage and assist needy children and parents under the new program to obtain education, training and employment needed to avoid long-term welfare dependence, and to make other necessary improvements to assure that the new program will be more effective in achieving its objectives.[9]

Title I of The Family Support Act strengthened laws and established new regulations mandating states to enforce the responsibility of absent parents to support their children. This title established guidelines for child-support award amounts, allowed for wage garnishment, established performance standards for state paternity programs, and provided for increased federal assistance for paternity establishment.

Title II created the Job Opportunities and Basic Skills Training Program, which provided a mandate for all states to administer education, job training, and employment programs, while Title III addressed the new consensus issues of mutual responsibility and family stability. This title guaranteed support services such as child care for individuals who participate in Title II activities and provided extended child care and medical assistance to all individuals who leave public assistance for employment.

Title IV addressed the new consensus issue of strengthening families by requiring all states to provide AFDC benefits to two-parent families. At the same time, Title V addressed the issue of state discretion by allowing states to conduct family support demonstration projects. These projects study the effect of early childhood development programs, test alternative definitions of unemployment, address child-care problems, expand the number of job opportunities available to certain low-income individuals, and provide counseling and other services to high-risk teenagers. Title VI contains miscellaneous provisions that pertain to American territories and administrative issues while Title VII contains the funding provisions.

Even though a "new consensus" about welfare reform had materialized, passage of the Family Support Act was the culmination of a long, protracted battle between the House, Senate, and the Reagan administration over the cost, potential benefits, and the JOBS requirements of Title II. Initially, President Reagan was so opposed to the concept that he threatened to veto the Senate bill, S1511, when it was first proposed by Senator Moynihan (D-NY) on July 21, 1987. At the time, the Reagan administration was more interested in pursuing the "New Federalism" doctrine—turning over responsibility for workfare programs to the states—than in increasing federal spending on new programs.

The major breakthrough probably came when the two key Republicans on the Senate Finance Committee, Senators Robert Dole (R-Kan.) and Robert Packwood (R-Ore.), voted in favor of the marked-up version of the bill in April 1988. After the markup session, Senator Packwood even predicted that the Senate would pass the Family Support Act by an 80–20 margin. Five months later, on September 29, 1988, the Senate passed the bill by a 96–1 vote. The next day the House passed the legislation by a vote of 347–53.

Despite being forced to soften its opposition to the bill, the White House won two significant changes to the JOBS portion of the initial legislation. The first amendment required at least one parent in a two-parent household receiving AFDC to be in some form of workfare for at least sixteen hours a week. The second change required the mandatory participation of at least 7 percent of each state's eligible AFDC population in fiscal years 1990 and 1991 increasing to 20 percent in fiscal year 1995.

Despite garnering a "new consensus" on welfare reform and overwhelming support in Congress, some conservative groups still differed with the philosophy of the Family Support Act. For instance, James Bovard with the Cato Institute in Washington, D.C., stated:

> The best change in the welfare system would be to lower benefits. That way welfare recipients would get jobs. It's not right to have some people working at $9.75 an hour and struggling to make ends meet, while down the street a neighbor is getting $7.00 an hour and not working.[10]

Stuart Butler with the Heritage Foundation in Washington, D.C., said "that while the Family Support Act is a step in the right direction,"[11] he was uncertain whether the law would actually reduce the welfare rolls. In fact, Butler pointed out that statistics released by the Congressional Budget Office indicate that the welfare rolls would actually increase in the coming years. This prediction by Butler proved to be quite accurate since AFDC caseloads have set record numbers since the passage of the Family Support Act.[12]

JOB OPPORTUNITIES AND BASIC SKILLS TRAINING PROGRAM

The major provision of the Family Support Act, and the one that seems to cause the most controversy is Title II, The Job Opportunities and Basic Skills Training Program, 45 CFR Part 205. "The purpose of the Job Opportunities and Basic Skills Training Program under Titles IV-A and IV-F of the Social Security Act is to assure that needy families with children obtain the education, training, and employment that will help avoid long-term welfare dependence."[13] To accomplish this purpose, the JOBS program has five stated objectives. Among them is to encourage, assist, and require recipients of AFDC to fulfill their responsibilities to support their children by preparing for, accepting, and retaining employment. Other objectives are to provide individuals with the opportunity to acquire the education and skills necessary to qualify for employment; to provide the necessary support services, including transitional child care and medical assistance, so that individuals can participate in JOBS and accept employment; to promote coordination of services at all levels of government in order to make a wide range of services available, particularly for individuals at risk of long-term welfare dependency; and finally, to emphasize accountability for both participants and service providers.

The JOBS program replaces and expands current authority for welfare education, training, and work programs contained in Title IV-A (AFDC) and Title IV-C (Work Incentive, or WIN, and WIN Demonstration Programs) of the Social Security Act. To correct for perceived problems of past programs, JOBS regulations require states to meet specific base enrollment and service levels or risk the possibility of losing federal matching funds. Each state was required to have a JOBS program in operation by October 1, 1990. Beginning on that date, states were required to have at least 7 percent of the state's mandatory AFDC recipients participating in JOBS program activities designed to last a minimum of twenty hours per week. On October 1, 1993, states must have enrolled 15 percent of the mandatory AFDC population, and by October 1, 1994, 20 percent of the state's mandatory AFDC recipients must be participating in JOBS.

In addition, states must spend their JOBS funds on individuals who are most in need and avoid the practice of "creaming participants" which often happened in past programs. States must spend 55 percent of their JOBS funds on potentially long-term dependent groups such as young mothers under age twenty-four who have not completed high school or the equivalent education and families that have received public assistance for thirty-six out of the last sixty months. Any state failing to meet the above requirements faces the possibility of having its federal matching funds reduced.

States also must offer an individually tailored package of services and benefits so that AFDC recipients may participate fully in JOBS. They must provide educational activities that promote basic literacy, and high school or equivalent education, in addition to a number of job-related activities such as job training, job preparation, and job-search assistance. States are also required to provide JOBS participants with support services such as child care, transportation assistance, health care, and counseling.

The JOBS legislation provides for mandatory participation unless the AFDC recipient has good cause for not participating. These reasons are generally related to having young children in the home, health problems, transportation problems, or a situation where the individual is needed in the home to care for an incapacitated relative. If AFDC recipients refuse to participate in JOBS without adequate cause, they can lose a portion of their AFDC grant. If welfare recipients complete JOBS and go to work, however, the state is required to provide twelve months of transitional child care and medical benefits to help ease their transition from welfare to employment.

There are several features unique to JOBS that make it different from WIN and other past employment and training programs. First of all, JOBS funding is higher than WIN funding and is more protected from cutbacks than WIN. Federal WIN funding was a discretionary grant to states and was gradually reduced from $395 million in fiscal year 1980 to $133 million in fiscal year 1987. In contrast, JOBS funding is a set capped entitlement that requires states to contribute matching funds. State funds are matched by federal funds at a rate from 50 to 90 percent, depending on how the funds are spent. The federal JOBS funding cap is set at $600 million for FY 1989, $800 million in FY 1990, $1 billion in FY 1991 through 1993, $1.1 billion in FY 1994, and $1.3 billion in FY 1995.[14]

JOBS also differs from WIN in the areas of education, targeting services, and requirements for coordination. One of the key features of

JOBS is its emphasis on providing educational services to AFDC recipients and provisions that allow states to mandate that teen parents participate in obtaining an education. In comparison, the main focus of WIN was job-search activities; WIN did not have an educational component. Unlike WIN, JOBS requires states to coordinate program activities with local Job Training Partnership Act Private Industry Councils (PIC), state departments of education, and the state employment service to avoid duplication of services.

JOBS contains one other key feature that was absent in the WIN program—an emphasis on the responsibility of government to provide the support services necessary to allow individuals to participate. These services include child care, transportation assistance, and providing reimbursement for expenses related to work and training. In addition, JOBS requires states to continue providing child care and medical assistance for a year after an individual becomes employed and leaves AFDC.

The following chart, 4-1, compares major JOBS provisions with those of other principal pre-JOBS federal employment and training programs.

THE MISSOURI JOBS PROGRAM

Missouri began its JOBS program on July 1, 1990, three months prior to the federal implementation deadline, in St. Louis City and twelve eastern Missouri counties. On July 1, 1991, Jackson, Clay, and Platte counties in the Kansas City area joined JOBS along with Lincoln and Pike counties in northeast Missouri. On January 1, 1992, four southwest Missouri counties in the Springfield area and three central Missouri counties in the Columbia-Jefferson City area joined JOBS. All remaining counties implemented JOBS programs between July 1, 1992, and October 1, 1992, the federal deadline for making the JOBS program available statewide. (See chart 4-2.)

Prior to implementing JOBS, Missouri operated a Work Incentive (WIN) program in St. Louis City and eight counties in southeast Missouri, also called the "Bootheel." In addition, Missouri operated two "Learnfare" projects under the auspices of WIN, in St. Louis City and Kansas City. Federal WIN program funding had been declining since the early 1980s forcing Missouri to incrementally reduce WIN program operations—which at one time included the St. Louis City and twenty-nine of the state's largest counties, accounting for approximately 84 percent of

CHART 4-1[15]

MAJOR AFDC WELFARE-TO-WORK PROVISIONS BEFORE AND AFTER JOBS

	BEFORE JOBS	UNDER JOBS
Program(s)	WIN, WIN-Demonstration, Job Search, Community Work Experience, Work Supplementation	JOBS
Administrative control	WIN: State AFDC agency and state employment service agency All others: State AFDC agency	State AFDC agency
Geographic coverage	Job Search: Statewide Other programs: Not required to be statewide	Statewide (by Oct. 1, 1992)
Required to participate	Generally: AFDC recipients aged 16–64 with children aged 6 or over; nonparent teens aged 16–18 and not in school	Generally: AFDC recipients aged 16–59 with children aged 3 or over; teen parents with children of any age; nonparent teens aged 16–18 and not in school
Participation requirements	WIN: Those required to participate were to be registered, but no participation rate was specified	For federal fiscal years 1990–91, 7 percent of those required to participate must average 20 hours in activities a week; this rises to 11 percent in 1992–93, 15 percent in 1994, and 20 percent in 1995
Targeting requirements	WIN: Priorities stated, but not enforced: 1. Unemployed parents who are principal earners in 2-parent families 2. Mothers who volunteer 3. Other mothers and pregnant women under the age of 19 who are required to participate 4. Dependent children and relatives aged 16 or over	At least 55 percent of JOBS funds must be spent on the following: 1. AFDC recipients or applicants who have received AFDC for any 36 months out of the past 5 years 2. AFDC parents under the age of 24 who (a) have not completed high school and are not enrolled in high school (or the equivalent) or (b) had little or no work experience in the preceding year 3. Members of AFDC families in which the youngest child will in 2 years be old enough to make the family ineligible for aid

CHART 4-1 *CONTINUED*

	BEFORE **JOBS**	UNDER **JOBS**
Activities	Could include, but not limited to, development of employability plan, job placement assistance, training, work experience, and subsidized employment	Must include assessment of employability, development of employability plan, education (high school, basic and remedial, English proficiency), job skills training, job readiness, and job development and placement Plus at least 2 optional activities: job search, work experience, on-the-job training, or work supplementation May include post-secondary education and other approved activities
Supportive services	Child care and other services needed to find employment or take training	Child care guaranteed if needed; transportation and other work-related assistance provided

SOURCE: U.S. General Accounting Office, *Welfare to Work: States Begin JOBS, But Fiscal and Other Problems May Impede Their Progress*, Table 1.1, GAO/HRD-91-106, Washington, D.C. (September 1991).

the state's AFDC population.[16]

 The final state WIN report, issued on June 30, 1990, indicated that during FY 1990, the eastern Missouri WIN program had served or registered 15,203 individuals. Of this total, 2,268 persons received some reportable service during the year besides registration. The services received most often were referral to support services (1,828 individuals) and counseling (1,795 individuals). In addition, 577 individuals were referred to employers for job interviews while 174 individuals were placed in jobs. The vast majority of the 15,303 WIN participants, 12,935 individuals, received no services from the WIN program other than registration during FY 1990.[17] These figures are probably characteristic of most late WIN programs and support earlier literature findings that WIN provided few real services and existed to mainly fulfill a federal work-registration requirement in its declining years. As Nancy Dickinson pointed out in "Which Welfare Strategies Work," WIN funding proved inadequate to meet federal registration requirements and provide quality services to

CHART 4-2

JOBS IMPLEMENTATION BY COUNTY, JULY 1, 1990–OCTOBER 1, 1992

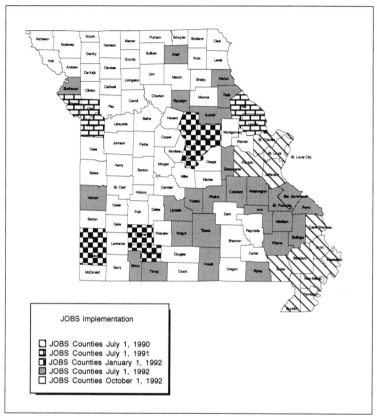

SOURCE: Missouri Department of Social Services, Division of Family Services

program participants; thus, it became mainly a registration requirement.[18]

In state fiscal year 1988, Missouri Governor Ashcroft directed several state agencies to cooperate in the design and administration of a special project to provide basic education services to AFDC recipients who had not completed high school. This project was called the Governor's Learnfare Initiative, or Learnfare. Learnfare was administered through the WIN program and consisted of two sites, one in St. Louis City and one in Kansas City. At its peak in FY 1990, the St. Louis Learnfare project registered 4,023 individuals but had provided service to only 778 participants. The Kansas City Learnfare project was designed to serve approximately thirty-five individuals at any point in time and a total of three hundred participants during FY 1990. Again, as with WIN, Learnfare had a large number of registrants in comparison to the number of individuals actually getting service.

While Learnfare operated under a very tight budget and was not designed to provide the same variety of services as JOBS eventually offered, the Learnfare projects allowed Missouri to experiment with educational programs for AFDC recipients and forced agencies to begin coordination efforts that would be continued with JOBS. These coordination efforts even included two private agencies, the Women's Employment Network in Kansas City and the Grace Hill Neighborhood Inc. in St. Louis, both of which provided services to Learnfare participants. On June 30, 1990, all WIN and Learnfare activities ended as JOBS became operational on July 1, 1990. One interesting note about WIN and Learnfare is that all active participants as of June 30, 1990, were provided the opportunity to transition into the JOBS program. Fewer than twenty WIN participants from the eastern Missouri counties, however, volunteered to join JOBS.

JOBS officially started in Missouri on July 1, 1990, three months before the final federal deadline of October 1, 1990. While Missouri could have implemented JOBS as early as July 1, 1989, the state delayed implementation because of state budget problems.[19] Planning for JOBS actually began in October 1989 when the state office administrative and planning staff was hired. On July 1, 1990, St. Louis City and the counties of St. Louis, St. Charles, Jefferson, Franklin, Cape Girardeau, Stoddard, Dunklin, Mississippi, Scott, New Madrid, Butler, and Pemiscot became the first Missouri JOBS counties.

Since all state JOBS programs have to be administered in accordance with the federal regulations contained in 45 CFR Part 205 and all states are required to have a state operations plan approved by the U.S. Department of Health and Human Services (HHS), Family Support Administration, the Missouri JOBS program is very similar to the JOBS programs of other states. But because of the flexibility allowed by the federal JOBS regulations, Missouri's JOBS program also has unique features.

During the design and planning phase of JOBS, Division of Family Services (DFS) JOBS staff met with various groups to gather input on program design and content. These groups included staff from other state agencies including the Missouri Departments of Education, Labor, and Economic Development. In addition, the JOBS staff met with local organizations such as the United Way, Salvation Army, Reform Organization for Welfare, several local Private Industry Councils, local school districts, local DFS staff, and other community groups. Also, DFS JOBS staff held public meetings, two of which were in locations where AFDC recipients could attend and provide input. Once a draft of the plan was available, it was released for public comment prior to being submitted to HHS. All in all, while the JOBS service delivery system was designed by state DFS staff, considerable outside input went into preparation of the state plan.[20]

Under the system that emerged, Missouri's JOBS program recruited potential participants using several methods. First, as JOBS became operational in an area, all AFDC recipients received information about the JOBS program in their monthly check and from their DFS Income Maintenance (IM) workers. Next, DFS used media advertising and local community groups, such as churches, the Salvation Army, local school districts, other government agencies, and not-for-profit organizations, as sources of JOBS referrals. Potential participants, referred by one of the above sources to the JOBS office, attended an orientation where the JOBS program was explained, and they learned what JOBS could do for them. Also, potential participants were informed of their rights and responsibilities under JOBS regulations since, technically, JOBS is a mandatory program and failure to participate could result in reduced public assistance benefits.

According to federal JOBS regulations, any AFDC recipient who does not have a child under the age of three and who does not have a good reason for not being able to participate in an appropriate educational, job-training, or job-readiness/job-search activity, is a mandatory JOBS participant and can be required to participate or lose a portion of public assistance benefits. AFDC recipients who are not mandatory participants are classified as exempt; however, the federal JOBS regulations require states to consider exempt volunteer JOBS participants first as long as states still meet their federal mandate that 55 percent of all individuals served come from the federally identified target groups. To date, Missouri has had more than enough volunteers for the JOBS program so it has not been necessary to take a "hard line" approach at calling in mandatory participants and forcing them to participate.

Today, potential participants complete orientation and volunteer for the JOBS program, they participate in assessment activities. They are tested to determine their educational achievement level and areas of employment interest in addition to determining their support service needs. They are then assigned to their individual JOBS case manager, who will work with them as long as they are in the program.

Each new JOBS participant and the case manager jointly complete an individual employability plan (IEP) which specifically describes what actions the AFDC recipient will take and which services the state will provide to help the individual participate fully in JOBS. The welfare recipient agrees to take certain actions while the state agrees to provide additional services such as case management, child care, transportation assistance, and medical assistance to allow the individual to participate. If mandatory participants fail to meet their obligations without good cause, they risk being sanctioned, i.e., having their benefits reduced. If the state fails to provide the assistance specified in the IEP, the participant has good cause for not participating in JOBS.

Once the IEP is agreed to, the case manager arranges for the necessary support services and a series of components designed to eliminate the participant's specific barriers to self-sufficiency. JOBS components could include activities such as life skills training, parenting classes, substance abuse programs, remedial educational activities including adult education classes or enrollment in high school, job training or vocational training, on-the-job training, job search and job readiness, or even post-secondary education activities in a college setting. The entire time a participant is in JOBS, the same case manager is available to help work on problems and facilitate his or her movement from one activity component to another. Because of the perceived importance of the case manager to the success of the JOBS participant, DFS adopted the recommendation of several groups that JOBS caseloads be kept relatively small, no more than thirty to thirty-five cases per case manager, one of the lower JOBS caseload standards in the nation.[21] This compares to DFS Income Maintenance caseloads that exceed two hundred AFDC recipients in some areas.[22]

The following chart, 4-3, displays the basic program flow and identifies the major organizations responsible for providing specific services. As this chart indicates, the DFS case manager is the central point in the process, controlling intake of participants and referral to components and the agencies providing these services. The Department of Elementary and Secondary Education, through local school districts, is the principal provider of basic education activities. The Division of Employment Security is the principal job-readiness/job-search provider, while the Job Training Partnership Act (JTPA) system coordinates most of the occupational and skill training activities. Other organizations are also available to provide needed services also.

As chart 4-3 indicates, the Missouri JOBS program followed federal guidelines to coordinate activities with other agencies in order to use

CHART 4-3

MISSOURI JOBS PROGRAM (PARTICIPANT FLOW)

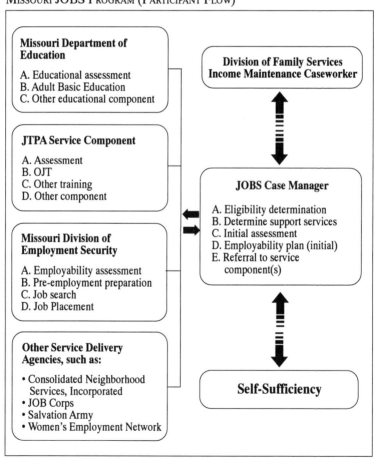

Missouri Department of Education

A. Educational assessment
B. Adult Basic Education
C. Other educational component

JTPA Service Component

A. Assessment
B. OJT
C. Other training
D. Other component

Missouri Division of Employment Security

A. Employability assessment
B. Pre-employment preparation
C. Job search
D. Job Placement

Other Service Delivery Agencies, such as:

• Consolidated Neighborhood Services, Incorporated
• JOB Corps
• Salvation Army
• Women's Employment Network

Division of Family Services Income Maintenance Caseworker

JOBS Case Manager

A. Eligibility determination
B. Determine support services
C. Initial assessment
D. Employability plan (initial)
E. Referral to service component(s)

Self-Sufficiency

available resources prior to setting up a new service delivery system and to avoid duplication.

The Missouri JOBS program exhibits some of the same trends that have been identified nationally. Like the rest of the nation, Missouri is moving away from relatively less intensive, low-cost services such as job search in favor of more intensive—and therefore more costly—education and training activities. On June 30, 1992, over 70 percent of all JOBS participants were in educational activities versus approximately 12 percent in job-search or job-readiness components.[23] Missouri offers several optional JOBS components such as life skills education, Parents as Teachers, on-the-job training, job search, and work experience. Post-secondary educational activities are an integral part of the Missouri JOBS program, accounting for 18.3 percent of the participant activities on June 30, 1992.[24]

LOCAL JOBS IMPLEMENTATION ENVIRONMENT

One of the unique features of the JOBS program and its enabling legislation is flexibility. This flexibility allows states to offer education, training, and employment activities that meet the specific needs of a particular area or population. Within the parameters of the legislation, local JOBS programs can be designed to address the diversity found in a state like Missouri which contains both major metropolitan areas and sparsely populated rural areas where local economies are dependent on a variety of different industries such as manufacturing, agriculture, and tourism. To control for Missouri's regional diversity, this study examined the JOBS program in the state's two metropolitan areas, St. Louis City and Kansas City/Jackson County, in Lincoln and Pike counties in rural northeast Missouri, and in eight rural counties in southeast Missouri. Each of these areas contains at least one unique feature that sets it apart from the other sites.

St. Louis City has several unique characteristics which make its JOBS program different from some of the other sites being studied. Many of the JOBS staff previously worked in the discontinued WIN and Learnfare programs, so they provided a core of experienced staff for building the JOBS program. The JOBS staff also had the advantage of previously working with many of the old WIN service delivery agencies, and had staff contacts and lines of communications already established. In addition, the St. Louis AFDC population is fairly concentrated in an area with a public transportation system as well as public and private education and training institutions.

When compared to rest of the state, however, the population and economy of St. Louis City is more impoverished and distressed. Data reflecting recent trends, moreover, indicate the city's economy is getting worse. For instance, between 1980 and 1990, the population of St. Louis City decreased by 12.4 percent while the percent of the people living in poverty increased from 21.4 percent to 24 percent, an increase of 2.6 percent. Over the past five years, the official unemployment rate has increased slightly from 6.6 percent in 1987 to 6.8 percent in 1991 after experiencing a low point of 5.5 percent in 1989. During the five-year period from 1986–1990, both the AFDC and food stamp caseloads have exhibited a steady growth, when calculated as a percent of the city's popu-

TABLE 4-1[25]

POPULATION AND POVERTY IN SELECTED COUNTIES

AREA	% POPULATION CHANGE 1980–1990	% Poverty Rate 1979	% Poverty Rate 1989	CHANGE
St. Louis City	-12.4	21.4	24.0	2.6
Jackson County	.6	10.9	12.8	1.9
Butler	2.8	23.8	24.5	0.7
Cape Girardeau	4.8	11.2	13.2	2.0
Dunklin	-8.8	23.4	29.3	5.9
Mississippi	-8.2	25.3	29.1	3.8
New Madrid	-8.8	27.0	26.4	-0.6
Pemiscot	-12.3	32.7	35.3	2.6
Scott	-0.7	16.5	18.1	1.6
Stoddard	-0.4	17.4	20.8	3.4
Lincoln	30.2	10.5	11.6	1.1
Pike	-9.1	17.1	17.7	0.6
Total Missouri	4.1	11.8	13.0	1.2

NOTE: Data are rounded.
SOURCE: U.S. Department of Commerce, Bureau of Census, Table 1, Selected Population and Housing Characteristics, 1990.

lation. The proportion of the St. Louis City population receiving AFDC increased from 13.1 percent in 1986 to 13.8 percent in 1990 while the proportion of the population receiving food stamps increased from 20.1 percent to 22.8 percent for the same time period. (See tables 4-1 through 4-4.)

The St. Louis City JOBS program began on July 1, 1990. Prior to JOBS, St. Louis City was the location of one of two active Work Incentive program sites and the primary site of the Governor's Learnfare Initiative. The St. Louis JOBS project was designed primarily by state office program planning staff with input from local community organizations and other government agencies that would be participating in the JOBS service delivery system. The St. Louis JOBS staff are under the direct

TABLE 4-2[26]

PERCENT UNEMPLOYMENT RATE FOR SELECTED COUNTIES, 1987–1991

AREA	1987	1988	1989	1990	1991
St. Louis City	6.6	6.0	5.5	5.9	6.8
Jackson County	6.7	6.0	5.7	5.4	6.5
Butler	9.7	8.6	8.5	7.4	8.3
Cape Girardeau	4.4	4.5	4.2	4.4	4.8
Dunklin	9.2	7.7	7.7	8.7	9.1
Mississippi	9.5	8.6	7.3	9.3	10.0
New Madrid	8.5	7.4	7.4	8.5	9.4
Pemiscot	8.8	8.0	7.8	8.5	9.4
Scott	7.8	7.0	6.6	7.4	8.9
Stoddard	9.4	8.1	7.2	8.0	9.0
Lincoln	8.5	7.5	6.9	7.2	8.6
Pike	8.8	7.4	7.3	7.2	7.4
Total Missouri	6.3	5.7	5.5	5.7	6.6

NOTE: Data are rounded.
SOURCE: Missouri Department of Labor and Industrial Relations, Division of Employment Security, Research and Analysis Section, October 1992.

supervision of a JOBS program manager located in the St. Louis area. The program manager reports directly to the JOBS program administrator (Division of Family Services, deputy division director for employment and training programs) in Jefferson City who reports to the director of the Division of Family Services.

The Kansas City/Jackson County JOBS program began on July 1, 1991.[29] Prior to JOBS, Kansas City was the location for one of two Governor's Learnfare Initiative projects. In contrast to the St. Louis City JOBS project, the Kansas City JOBS service delivery system was designed entirely by a group of local citizens who represented community and business organizations and the local government agencies that would be participating in the JOBS service delivery system. Gary Stangler, the

TABLE 4-3[27]

PERCENT OF POPULATION RECEIVING AFDC IN SELECTED COUNTIES, 1986–1990

AREA	1986	1987	1988	1989	1990
St. Louis City	13.0	13.0	13.3	13.5	13.8
Jackson County	4.2	4.2	4.3	4.6	4.9
Butler	7.3	7.6	8.0	8.0	7.6
Cape Girardeau	2.4	2.5	2.5	2.7	2.8
Dunklin	10.9	11.3	10.9	10.2	10.8
Mississippi	12.3	11.8	11.4	11.3	11.7
New Madrid	11.2	11.0	11.0	11.0	10.6
Pemiscot	15.0	15.6	15.0	14.7	15.4
Scott	7.1	7.0	6.6	6.8	7.1
Stoddard	5.3	5.8	5.4	5.1	4.9
Lincoln	2.0	2.0	2.0	2.2	2.5
Pike	5.2	5.1	4.7	4.5	4.3
Total Missouri	4.0	4.0	4.0	4.0	4.1

NOTE: Data are rounded.
SOURCE: Missouri Department of Social Services, Research and Evaluation, *Division of Family Services Annual Report for Fiscal Year 1991*, Table 1.

director of the Missouri Department of Social Services, appointed the members of the Kansas City JOBS committee and offered the "complete support of the Department of Social Services in order to make the Kansas City JOBS project the best in the country."[30]

The Kansas City JOBS program is structured in a way very similar to that of St. Louis. JOBS staff are under the direct supervision of a JOBS program manager located in the Kansas City area. The program manager reports directly to the JOBS program administrator in Jefferson City. The Kansas City JOBS committee acts in an advisory and oversight role, meeting quarterly to review the progress of the JOBS program. The committee chairperson is available practically full time to consult with state JOBS staff; one state employee serves as staff support for the committee.

TABLE 4-4[28]

PERCENT OF POPULATION RECEIVING FOOD STAMPS IN SELECTED COUNTIES, 1986–1990

AREA	1986	1987	1988	1989	1990
St. Louis City	20.1	19.9	20.6	21.7	22.8
Jackson County	6.6	6.4	6.8	7.9	8.6
Butler	16.4	17.2	17.5	17.9	17.4
Cape Girardeau	5.2	5.2	5.6	6.0	6.5
Dunklin	22.4	23.0	22.3	22.2	23.5
Mississippi	27.6	26.9	25.9	25.7	26.8
New Madrid	24.1	22.5	21.7	21.7	22.1
Pemiscot	31.2	31.9	30.5	30.5	31.6
Scott	14.8	14.4	14.3	14.6	14.7
Stoddard	14.2	14.3	13.4	13.1	12.9
Lincoln	4.8	4.3	4.7	5.1	5.5
Pike	10.8	10.0	9.7	9.1	9.2
Total Missouri	7.6	7.6	7.6	7.9	8.3

NOTE: Data are rounded.
SOURCE: Missouri Department of Social Services, Research and Evaluation, *Division of Family Services Annual Report for Fiscal Year 1991*, Table 33.

Besides being designed by a committee of local citizens, the Kansas City project has several unique features which make its JOBS program different from the other sites in Missouri. First of all, the staff hired for JOBS was completely new, and most had never worked with employment and training programs. For the most part, JOBS staff had to establish linkages and working relationships with the service delivery agencies that would be cooperating with JOBS; however, some of the agencies were represented on the advisory committee.

From the beginning, the JOBS committee insisted on innovations unique to Kansas City. Members of the committee representing the Ewing Kaufmann Foundation and the Women's Employment Network had previously worked with staff from the University of Kansas at Lawrence (KU) to develop a case management model and life-skills training curriculum for their programs. The committee directed that the JOBS program adopt the KU case management model and life-skills curriculum for use in the Kansas City program. Staff from the University of Kansas were hired to provide training to the JOBS staff and act as consultants.

In addition, the advisory committee functions in an oversight and evaluation role. It has developed an interest in program outcome measures other than the population participation and target group participation percentages required by the Department of Health and Human Services. For example, local JOBS management staff are periodically required to provide the advisory committee with data about caseload levels, the number of JOBS graduates entering employment, employment wage rates, and job retention rates. This aspect of the committee's involvement appears to have "focused" the Kansas City JOBS staff's attention on employment-related outcomes. In other words, the committee is evaluating JOBS from the business perspective of wanting to see a positive return on its investment.

Fortunately, the Jackson County population and economy does not appear to be as impoverished or distressed as that of St. Louis. For instance, between 1980 and 1990 the population of Jackson County increased by .6 percent while the percentage of the people living in poverty increased from 10.9 percent to 12.8 percent, a change of almost 2 percent. Over the past five years, the official unemployment rate has decreased slightly from 6.7 percent in 1987 to 6.5 percent in 1991 experiencing a low point of 5.4 percent in 1990. During the five-year period from 1986 to 1990, both the AFDC and food stamp caseloads have exhibited a slow growth when calculated as a percent of the county's population. The proportion of the Jackson County population receiving AFDC increased from 4.2 percent in 1986 to 4.9 percent in 1990 while the proportion of the population receiving food stamps increased from 6.6 percent to 8.6 percent for the same time period. (See tables 4-1 through 4-4.)

The southeast Missouri, or Bootheel, JOBS program consists of Butler, Cape Girardeau, Dunklin, Mississippi, New Madrid, Pemiscot, Scott, and Stoddard counties. All eight counties began their JOBS programs on July 1, 1990. Prior to JOBS, the Bootheel was the location of one of two active Work Incentive program sites. The Bootheel JOBS program was designed primarily by state office program planning staff with input from local community organizations and other government agencies that would be participating in the JOBS service delivery system. Unlike St. Louis and Kansas City, the Bootheel JOBS staff are under the direct supervision of the Division of Family Services area director for southeast Missouri and receive program support and technical assistance from the JOBS program manager located in the St. Louis area. The area director reports directly to the director of the Division of Family Services.

Besides the difference in staff supervision and organizational structure, the Bootheel has several features which make its JOBS program different from the metropolitan programs. The first and most unique element is that the Bootheel is generally rural. While the area does contain several large towns such as Cape Girardeau (population 34,438), Poplar Bluff (population 16,996), and Sikeston (population 17,641), the eight-county Bootheel site is predominantly rural with an economy dependent on agriculture and agricultural services.[31] The Bootheel lacks some features found in the metropolitan areas conducive to the operation of employment and training programs, specifically, a widespread public transportation system and a variety of social service providers. The rural nature of many Bootheel counties combined with the absence of public transportation outside of major towns presents a problem for AFDC recipients who would like to take advantage of JOBS services but who do not have reliable transportation.

The population and economy of the Bootheel is quite diverse. For instance, some areas of the region have a strong economy such as Cape Girardeau County with an unemployment rate of 4.8 percent, 13.2 percent of the population living in poverty, 2.8 percent of the population receiving AFDC, and 6.5 percent of the population receiving food stamps. Yet, some of the other counties in the region have traditionally been some of the poorest counties in the state.

For instance, in Pemiscot County 35.3 percent of the population lives in poverty while over 29 percent of the population of Dunklin and Mississippi counties lives below the poverty level. In Pemiscot County, 15.4 percent of the population receives AFDC while 31.6 percent receives food stamps and 9.4 percent of the population is unemployed. With the exception of Cape Girardeau, the Bootheel counties all have unemployment rates, poverty rates, and public assistance rates that exceed the state average. (See tables 4-1 through 4-4.)

The northeast Missouri JOBS site, consisting of Lincoln and Pike counties, became operational on July 1, 1991. While relatively small, it is one of the more unique JOBS sites in the state. What makes the Lincoln/Pike project unique is that the JOBS case manager is co-located with staff from several state agencies at the vocational-technical school in the small town of Eolia, Missouri. This is the only JOBS site in Missouri where all program activities are provided at one location. JOBS participants can meet with their DFS case manager, participate in Adult Basic Education or vocational training activities provided by the Department of Elementary and Secondary Education, or obtain job-readiness and job-search assistance from a job service technician who is employed by the Division of Employment Security. In addition, program participants are able to ride the school buses, and child care is available close to the training center.

The organizational and supervisory structure in northeast Missouri is similar to that of the Bootheel with JOBS staff reporting to the DFS area director and receiving program support and technical assistance from the JOBS program manager located in Jefferson City. Like the Bootheel counties, Lincoln and Pike Counties are rural and the economy is highly dependent on agriculture and agricultural services. The largest town in the two-county area is Louisiana with a population of approximately 4,200 people. As tables 4-1 through 4-4 indicate, the population and economy of Lincoln County is slightly better off than Pike County. For instance, recent poverty data indicate that 11.6 percent of Lincoln County's population live below the poverty line while 2.5 percent receive AFDC and 5.5 percent receive food stamps. In Pike County, 17.7 percent of the population live in poverty while 4.3 percent receive AFDC and 9.2 percent receive food stamps. Lincoln County, however, has an 8.6 percent unemployment rate compared with 7.4 percent for Pike County,

As tables 4-1 through 4-4 indicate, there is a considerable difference in JOBS program design, staff organizational structure, and local economic conditions among the four sites chosen for this study. Both urban and rural JOBS sites are represented; the study also encompasses programs primarily designed by state planning staff and programs designed by local citizens; and some of the areas represented in this study have fairly strong economic indicators while others have traditionally been the most economically distressed counties in the state.

According to Gary Stangler, director of the Missouri Department of Social Services, the perfect time to start a new employment and training program for welfare recipients is when the economy is expanding and enough good jobs are being created to absorb all the people who want to go to work. Unfortunately, as the above data indicate, when JOBS started on July 1, 1990, Missouri's economy, like the nation's, was in recession, and the public assistance rolls in both Missouri and the United States were approaching record levels.

NOTES

1.   George Bush, "State of the Union Address," January 28, 1992.
2.   Robert D. Reischauer, "Welfare Reform: Will Consensus Be Enough?" *The Brookings Review* (Summer 1987), 3–8.
3.   For a discussion of the importance of research findings on welfare reform legislation see, Peter L. Szanton, "The Remarkable 'Quango': Knowledge, Politics, and Welfare Reform," *Journal of Policy Analysis and Management* 10, (1991): 590–602; and Erica B. Baum, "When the Witch Doctors Agree: The Family Support Act and Social Science Research," *Journal of Policy Analysis and Management* 10 (1991): 603–615.
4.   See Lawrence Mead, *Beyond Entitlement* (New York: The Free Press, 1986); and State of New York, *A New Social Contract: Report of the New York Task Force on Poverty and Welfare* (December 1986).
5.   State of New York, *A New Social Contract: Report of the New York Task Force on Poverty and Welfare.*
6.   Reischauer, "Welfare Reform: Will Consensus Be Enough?" 3–8.
7.   Ibid.
8.   Ibid., also see Julie Rovner, "Welfare Reform: The Issue That Bubbled Up from the States to Capitol Hill," *Governing* 2 (December 1988): 17–21.
9.   U.S. Congress, *Public Law 100-485*, 102 STAT.2343.
10.   Manpower Information Inc., *Employment and Training Reporter* (September 27, 1989), 58–64.
11.   Ibid.
12.   Ibid.
13.   U.S. Statutes at Large, Vol. 102: 2343. Also see U.S. Congress, *Public Law 100-485*.
14.   Manpower Information Inc., *Employment and Training Reporter*, 58–64.
15.   U.S. General Accounting Office, *Welfare to Work: States Begin JOBS, But Fiscal and Other Problems May Impede Their Progress*, GAO/HRD-91-106, (Washington, D.C., September 1991), 12.
16.   Julian Hargas, Former State WIN Program Supervisor, Missouri Department of Labor and Industrial Relations, Division of Employment Security, interview with author, 9 September 1992.

17. Missouri Department of Labor and Industrial Relations, Division of Employment Security, *ESARS Report*, A22, June 30, 1990, WIN Project 8600.

18. Nancy S. Dickinson, "Which Welfare Strategies Work?" *Social Work* 31 (July/August 1986): 267.

19. Greg Vadner, Deputy Director for Income Maintenance, Missouri Department of Social Services, Division of Family Services, interview with author, 17 June 1992.

20. Ibid.

21. Carmen K. Schulze, Director, Missouri Division of Family Services, Department of Social Services, interview with author, 10 September 1992.

22. Greg Vadner, interview, 1992.

23. Missouri Division of Family Services, *FUTURES Monthly Management Information Report*, June 30, 1992.

24. Ibid.

25. U.S. Department of Commerce, Bureau of Census, Table 1, "Selected Population and Housing Characteristics," 1990.

26. Missouri Department of Labor and Industrial Relations, Division of Employment Security, Research and Analysis Section, *Civilian Labor Force, Employment, Unemployment and Unemployment Rates* (October 1992).

27. Missouri Department of Social Services, Division of Family Services, *Fiscal Year 1991 Annual Report*, Table 1, 1.

28. Ibid., Table 33, 32.

29. While we refer to the project as Kansas City, the project covers all of Jackson County. Statistical data are for Jackson County.

30. Gary Stangler, Director of the Missouri Department of Social Services, during a presentation at the first meeting of the Kansas City JOBS committee, 18 January 1991.

31. U.S. Department of Commerce, Bureau of the Census, Table 1, Selected Population and Housing Characteristics.

V

The Job Opportunities and Basic Skills Training Program: Characteristics of Participants

> Since I've been back in school, I've realized I have the brains and ability to learn anything I want. I've enjoyed going to school and learning again. Most of my grades have been in the 90s. Now I feel better about myself and I know I will make it. If it weren't for the JOBS program and JTPA, I wouldn't have been able to do this.
>
> —Debbie, from Scott County[1]

Debbie is typical of many of the women receiving Aid to Families with Dependent Children (AFDC) grants in Missouri. She and her younger brother lived in poverty during much of her childhood; her family received food stamps as well as intermittent welfare in the form of AFDC. In addition, her family received occasional help from relatives, community groups, and the local Baptist church. Her biological father deserted the family when Debbie was nine years old, failing to provide any child support. Her mother lived with a succession of "boyfriends" while working in numerous jobs characterized by low skills, low wages, and no employee benefits such as health insurance. She never held these jobs for long.

For her part, Debbie did not like school and was never a good student. She was two years behind other children her age when she became pregnant at seventeen and dropped out of school. She married the child's father, who was also a high school dropout; she had a second child one year later and a third two years after that. Her life after marriage seemed to follow the same pattern as that of her mother. Her family received food stamps while she and her husband both worked a succession of low-skill, minimum-wage jobs, supplemented with public assistance and unemployment compensation. Approximately three years ago, Debbie's husband deserted the family and moved out of state. After her husband left Debbie and their three children, she became more dependent on the public assistance system.

Debbie, then twenty-nine, had always wanted to work, but felt her education and skill level only qualified her for minimum-wage jobs paying little more than the welfare system. She was also deterred by the need to pay for child care, transportation expenses, and clothing for work; moreover, she would have lost her Medicaid coverage even though she probably would not have obtained medical coverage from an employer.

In January 1991, Debbie entered the Missouri JOBS program where she completed her high school equivalency through the Adult Basic Education program and received her General Educational Development (GED) diploma. Next she entered a JTPA skill-training program to become a certified emergency medical technician with the career goal of working for a hospital as a member of an ambulance crew. Debbie is presently employed with a hospital in southeast Missouri where she earns about seven dollars an hour with a good employee-benefit package. The JOBS program will continue providing child care, on a sliding fee schedule, for one year from the date that Debbie left AFDC and started working.

Stories like Debbie's are quite common in the Missouri JOBS program and in JOBS programs operated by other states. Previous employment and training programs such as the Work Incentive program (WIN), the Comprehensive Employment and Training Act (CETA) programs, and the Job Training Partnership Act (JTPA) programs could also provide numerous individual success stories demonstrating the effectiveness of their services at moving people from dependency to the labor market. Yet, although anecdotal stories like Debbie's are interesting, they provide little hard information about the real effectiveness of employment and training programs at reducing welfare dependency, nor do they address the key concerns of many policymakers.

For instance, policymakers are concerned about whether employment and training programs serve the population most in need of the services. How effective employment and training programs are at reducing public assistance dependency is also an area of inquiry. Another question is whether employment and training programs for AFDC recipients are cost-effective. These are important questions because clients and taxpayers alike deserve cost-effective services that reach people with the most need.

RESEARCH QUESTIONS

To initiate our inquiry into the effectiveness of the Missouri JOBS program, chapter 5 will focus on which segment of the population is served by JOBS. As stated earlier, employment and training programs such as WIN, CETA, and JTPA have been criticized for the practice of "creaming participants"—enrolling people in their programs with a high potential for success while ignoring more-needy individuals.[2] To minimize the practice of creaming under JOBS, Congress included a requirement that state JOBS programs must spend 55 percent of their resources on individuals in three hard-to-serve target groups or have their federal matching funds reduced.

To determine the effectiveness of the Missouri JOBS program at serving the AFDC population, including the most needy, the following research questions and related null hypotheses will be studied and tested. (These research questions pertain to the demographics of AFDC and JOBS recipients; other research questions pertaining to outcomes will be presented in chapter 6.)

Research Question 1: Are the most dependent AFDC recipients receiving JOBS employment and training services?

Hypothesis 1: The most dependent individuals are less likely to receive JOBS services—JOBS is "creaming" participants.

Hypothesis 2: The percent of target group individuals in JOBS is less than the percent of target group individuals represented in the general AFDC population.

Research Question 2: Are JOBS participants representative of the AFDC population?

Hypothesis 3: There is no statistically significant difference between the characteristics of JOBS participants—such as education, length of time on welfare, age, work experience, race, and sex—and those of AFDC recipients who did not participate in JOBS.

DATA OVERVIEW

To examine the above research questions relating to the demographic attributes of the JOBS population compared to the general AFDC population and their extent of dependency and need for employment and training services, inquiry will focus on data maintained by the Missouri Department of Social Services (DSS) and the Division of Family Services (DFS) in their automated Income Maintenance and JOBS data systems. The DFS data systems contain individual records on all clients receiving services from the division, and they include client information such as age, sex, race, education level, work history, family composition information, reasons for entering and leaving the AFDC system, and client benefit information such as AFDC grant amount, non-AFDC reported income, source of income, and changes in AFDC eligibility status.

These systems are used primarily for processing AFDC benefit claims, compiling federal and state reports, facilitating caseworker activities, and maintaining historical records for audit and performance reviews. The DFS data are accessible by both social security account number and by a unique department client number (DCN). These data are considered quite accurate because they are used to determine program eligibility and for benefit disbursement. In addition, they are subject to periodic audit and validation by staff from several federal and state agencies including the U.S. Department of Health and Human Services (HHS), the Missouri State Auditor, the Department of Social Services' Division of Budget and Finance, and the Division of Family Services' Quality Control Section.

To assist with this study, the Division of Family Services allowed access to the individual records of all JOBS participants active in the program between July 1, 1990, and June 30, 1992. These individuals were labeled as the experimental group.[3] This study also used similar records for a sample of AFDC recipients from the same time period who were not in the JOBS program—who were labeled the comparison group. Staff from the Department of Social Services' Research and Evaluation Section selected the sample of comparison group subjects at random, using the Statistical Analysis System (SAS), from the universe of all the individuals who received cash AFDC benefits between July 1, 1990, and June 30, 1992, and who did not participate in JOBS. The experimental group contained 5,935 subjects while the comparison group contained 5,848 subjects. Utilizing SAS, DSS staff created the JOBS Research Data Set used for this study. (See appendix A for a list of data elements contained in the JOBS Research Data Set and their definitions.)

AFDC CHARACTERISTIC DATA— WHO IS BEING SERVED BY JOBS?

Individual characteristics can be used to provide an indication of group homogeneity and an individual's potential for employment and welfare dependency. For instance, previously cited research by noted poverty and social policy scholars Greg Duncan, Saul Hoffman, Mary Jo Bane, David Ellwood, Irwin Garfinkel, and Sara McLanahan indicates that certain individual attributes such as low educational attainment, low skill level, poor work history, and early child bearing predispose a person to a greater chance of public assistance dependency, especially when these attributes are combined with societal barriers such as racial prejudice.[4]

To examine our first research question—Are the most dependent AFDC recipients receiving JOBS employment and training services?— we will compare the key characteristics of JOBS and non-JOBS subjects that theoretically indicate a propensity for dependency. The characteristics chosen for comparison were selected with the assistance of several state office JOBS policy staff who were asked to select key individual characteristics from those available on the JOBS Research Data Set that they felt would provide an indication of group dependency and homogeneity.

Summary data describing the characteristic mean or the percentage of the key characteristic contained in the JOBS and non-JOBS populations were then reviewed by twenty-five JOBS staff who were selected at random and interviewed either at their work site or over the telephone. Staff were asked to evaluate the eight characteristics listed on table 5-1 and give their opinion about the characteristic's impact on the dependency of the JOBS participants in relation to the non-JOBS subjects. Based on the staff's experiences, they were asked to evaluate the difference in each characteristic's descriptive statistic and whether it has a meaningful impact on dependency. The difference was recorded as positive or negative; if staff felt there was no difference, this was indicated as neutral.

As table 5-1 indicates, the only attribute possessed by JOBS participants which was considered positive in relation to the non-JOBS subjects was education. The age attribute was considered neutral by most staff while all other attributes were considered negative—that is, in relation to the non-JOBS population, JOBS participants are perceived as possessing "less desirable" characteristics which make them harder to serve.

With regard to age, JOBS staff felt it was more difficult to place the younger women (under age twenty) and the older JOBS participants

TABLE 5-1

CHARACTERISTICS SELECTED FOR ANALYSIS OF GROUP HOMOGENEITY
AND IMPACT ON DEPENDENCY

VARIABLE	JOBS MEAN	NON-JOBS MEAN	JOBS STAFF ASSESSMENT OF IMPACT ON DEPENDENCY *(number of responses)*		
			Positive	Negative	Neutral
Age *(years)*	24.66	27.96	6	5	14
Education *(years)*	11.18	11.09	16	0	9
Work Experience *(last 12 mos.)*	2.48	0	0	17	8
Age at First Birth *(years)*	19.73	21.42	0	19	6
Time on AFDC *(months)*	32.73	29.56	0	18	7
Number of Children	2.20	2.10	0	14	11
Percent Minority	67.1	66.4	2	14	9
Percent Women	97.5	94.5	3	13	9

NOTE: JOBS staff were asked to assess each characteristic regarding its impact on dependency in relation to the non-JOBS group mean.

(over forty) especially if they been receiving welfare for any length of time. Generally, staff felt that difference in the mean age between JOBS and non-JOBS subjects was not a particular advantage for either group since the average participants in both groups were in their prime working years. Some staff indicated younger AFDC recipients would be the most difficult to work with because they generally had younger children, and they lacked maturity and work experience. Others felt older participants were harder to get into the labor market because they have adjusted to living on welfare and they view welfare as an alternative to working. In general, there was agreement this attribute lacked substantive significance.

Most JOBS staff believed that education was a key indicator of an individual's employability. They felt that lack of a high school diploma or its equivalent reduced a person's employability. While several staff felt there was no real difference between the mean educational attainment of the JOBS group with 11.18 grades of school completed and that of the non-JOBS group with 11.09 grades completed, there was general agreement that more education enhanced a person's chances of obtaining employment; however, we question whether the difference in group means is substantively significant.

Work experience is another characteristic JOBS staff perceived as an important indicator of self-sufficiency. Staff indicated that the majority of welfare recipients work intermittently, mixing welfare income with labor force earnings; however, they felt many of the AFDC recipients did not have jobs that paid enough to keep them off welfare. These jobs are often part-time or of short duration; also, individuals often quit because they are unable to combine work and motherhood on limited financial resources.

Staff members felt that the AFDC recipients most likely to become self-sufficient were the ones that either worked regularly or who were in school. They believed insufficient work experience was a real barrier to employment. In addition, staff personnel felt that potential employers would be reluctant to hire persons who were on welfare and who had not attempted to work or increase their education or job skills. They noted employers would view these individuals as indolent and a bad risk.

Interestingly, JOBS participants worked 2.48 months in the twelve months prior to June 30, 1992, while non-JOBS subjects averaged 2.92 months of work in the same time period. These data support the perceptions of the JOBS staff and research by Greg Duncan and Saul Hoffman, which was cited earlier, indicating the total package of resources available to AFDC recipients frequently includes a mix of both earned income and public assistance.[5] Again, we question the substantive significance of this variable.

Another characteristic that appears to be an indicator of potential poverty and dependency is the mother's age at the time of the birth of her first child. JOBS staff agreed that single parenthood at an early age was a negative attribute, especially when the first child was followed by a second child. Research indicates that early onset of sexual activity and child-bearing, especially for a single mother, exhibits a strong positive correlation with poverty and welfare dependency.[6] In addition, research conducted by the Missouri Department of Social Services indicates approximately one-half of all women receiving AFDC in Missouri had their first child as a teenager compared to 25 percent for the general population.[7] JOBS participants had their first child at a slightly younger age than non-JOBS subjects, 19.73 years of age versus 21.42 years.

JOBS staff indicated that length of time on AFDC is another good predictor of potential welfare dependency, if not the best indicator, and felt that the longer a person received public assistance the harder it would be to help them get out of the system. Staff felt that if a person becomes accustomed to living in the "welfare system" and learns to survive on what the state pays and "work the system," AFDC recipients become "comfortable" and the thought of leaving the system causes anxiety. Staff stated that long-time AFDC recipients know what to expect from the welfare system, and while it is not a great lifestyle, they feel it is better than the unknown.

Research findings by poverty researchers Greg Duncan and Saul Hoffman support the JOBS staff perceptions. They found that the average AFDC recipient spent less than two years on public assistance, but when they examined the AFDC caseload at one point in time, over one-half of the individuals receiving assistance were in the midst of a spell that would last eight years or more. They felt that one of the best predictors of future dependency was length of time the recipient had already received AFDC.[8] As table 5-2 indicates, JOBS participants received AFDC for an average of 32.79 months compared to 29.56 months for the non-JOBS group.

According to JOBS staff, the number of children in the AFDC family is another important indicator of dependency or potential dependency. Staff representatives felt there is a strong relationship between the number of children in the family and the AFDC recipient's ability to find a job with wages high enough to allow them to leave welfare. The most common observation was that even after completing high school or job training, JOBS graduates find employment in entry-level positions. It is very hard for a single mother with several children to sever her ties with the welfare system when she earns entry-level wages of less than six dollars an hour. This is especially difficult if the employer does not provide health benefits. As table 5-2 indicates, JOBS participants have slightly more children—2.20 per family—than non-JOBS subjects, who average 2.10 children per family. Again, we question if the difference represents substantive significance.

Staff respondents also perceived members of minority groups as being harder to serve then non-minority welfare recipients. Slightly more JOBS participants were members of a minority group (67.1 percent) than non-JOBS subjects (66.4 percent). Most staff attributed this perceived phenomenon to societal prejudices regarding race, in particular the prejudices of employers. These staff felt that the racial attribute alone made it

TABLE 5-2

IMPACT ON DEPENDENCY

VARIABLE	JOBS SUBJECTS MEAN	NON-JOBS SUBJECTS MEAN	DIFF. (+/-)	IMPACT ON DEPENDENCY
AGE	24.66	27.96	-3.30 YRS	NEUTRAL
EDUCATION	11.18	11.09	+0.09 YRS	POSITIVE
WORK EXP.	2.48	2.92	-0.44 MOS	NEGATIVE
AGE/FIRST BIRTH	19.73	21.42	-1.69 YRS	NEGATIVE
TIME ON AFDC	32.79	29.56	+3.23 MOS	NEGATIVE
NO. OF CHILDREN	2.20	2.10	+0.10 CHILD	NEGATIVE
MINORITY	67.1%	66.4%	+.70%	NEGATIVE
WOMEN	97.5%	94.5%	+3.00%	NEGATIVE

SOURCE: Missouri Department of Social Services, Research and Evaluation, JOBS Research Data Set and results from author's survey of JOBS staff.

harder for the JOBS participant to obtain employment, especially in better jobs.

When the minority characteristic is combined with single parent status and the "welfare" label, staff felt that many employers would perceive an individual as "damaged goods." Interestingly, a number of staff indicated they believed some of the contractual service providers—organizations outside the Department of Social Services—discriminated against the minority AFDC recipients in subtle ways such as not encouraging them to enter the better training programs or not referring them to better employers. One staff official recalled this remark made by an Adult Basic Education director from southeast Missouri during the early phases of JOBS: "These people don't need an education, they need to get a job and have less kids."[9] We do not feel the difference between the two groups is substantively significant.

As would be expected since the majority of AFDC recipients are women (94.5 percent), the overwhelming majority of JOBS participants are also women (97.5 percent). Staff observed that the majority of people receiving AFDC have problems that keep them from working, but few men face the problem of being a single parent. Most men in the program are from the two-parent Unemployed Parent (UP) assistance group. The men do not have the same family demands as the women, such as primary responsibility for taking care of sick children, so men's participation in JOBS is subject to less disruption from child-care problems. In addition, JOBS staff felt that the labor market discriminates against women and that there are more opportunities for men to obtain a higher paying job with a better future. Overall, the staff felt that the combination of responsibility for primary child care and discrimination in the labor market made it more difficult for women JOBS participants to succeed. Again, it is questionable if this difference between the two groups is substantively significant.

The recurring theme from our interviews with the JOBS staff was that one barrier to success did not cause an insurmountable problem. The individuals with whom staff work, however, often possess numerous attributes that make it more difficult for them to participate fully in JOBS and to obtain and keep employment after they complete the JOBS program. For example, JOBS participants are often black single mothers who have several children, who have not completed high school, and who have little meaningful work history and the added stigma of being welfare recipients.

FEDERAL TARGET GROUPS

Another way of looking at the issue of who is being served by JOBS is to examine the representation of federal target group individuals in the JOBS and non-JOBS population. As discussed earlier, to minimize the "creaming" phenomena, the JOBS legislation mandates that a minimum of 55 percent of all JOBS funds be spent on three hard-to-serve target groups in danger of potential long-term welfare dependency. The three groups are AFDC recipients who are under the age of twenty-four and who have not completed high school, AFDC recipients who have received benefits in thirty-six out of the previous sixty months, and AFDC recipients who are in danger of losing eligibility because their youngest child is within two years of reaching eighteen years of age.

Approximately 72 percent of all Missouri JOBS participants belonged to one of these three target groups. Almost 55 percent of the JOBS group had received AFDC in thirty-six of the last sixty months while approximately 17 percent were under twenty-four and had not finished high school. Of JOBS participants, 1 percent were about to lose AFDC eligibility because of the age of their youngest child. In comparison, approximately 45 percent of the non-JOBS subjects belonged to a target group. Almost 36 percent of the non-JOBS group had been on AFDC thirty-six out of the last sixty months, while almost 9 percent were under age twenty-four and had not finished high school. Data were not available about the age of the youngest child for members of this group.[10]

As table 5-3 indicates, there is considerable variance among the four regions with regard to the number of target group individuals in the JOBS population and in the non-JOBS AFDC population. For instance, St. Louis City has the highest proportion of target group individuals in both the JOBS and non-JOBS populations—72.2 percent versus 44.6 percent, while northeast Missouri has the smallest target group representation with 54 percent of the JOBS and 25.7 percent of the non-JOBS subjects belonging to one of the target groups. In all areas, the majority of the target group individuals were receiving AFDC for at least thirty-six of the last sixty months.

Interestingly, the proportion of target group individuals in the JOBS population significantly exceeds the proportion of target group individuals in the non-JOBS population in all four regions. Using the Statistical Analysis System, we constructed a table and performed a Chi-square test of significance on the statewide data, comparing the target group indi-

TABLE 5-3

PERCENT OF TARGET GROUP INDIVIDUALS BY REGION*

AREA	JOBS SUBJECTS			NON-JOBS SUBJECTS		
	N	TARGET GROUP	%	N	TARGET GROUP	%
TOTAL	5,537	3,998	72.2	5,848	2,610	44.6
36/60 Mos.		3,021	54.6		2,104	36.0
AGE, NO H.S.		921	16.6		506	8.
LOSE ELIGIBIL.		56	1.0		NA	NA
NOT TARGET		1,539	27.8		3,238	55.4
ST. LOUIS	2,899	2,269	78.3	2,579	1,390	53.9
36/60 Mos.		1,721	59.4		1,173	45.5
AGE, NO H.S.		518	17.9		217	8.4
LOSE ELIGIBIL.		30	1.0		NA	NA
NOT TARGET		630	21.7		1,189	46.1
KANSAS CITY	921	598	64.9	2,124	822	38.7
36/60 Mos.		449	48.8		638	30.0
AGE, NO H.S.		142	15.4		184	8.7
LOSE ELIGIBIL.		7	.8		NA	NA
NOT TARGET		323	35.1		1,302	61.3
NORTHEAST	76	41	54.0	101	26	25.7
36/60 Mos.		27	35.5		19	18.8
AGE, NO H.S.		12	15.8		7	6.9
LOSE ELIGIBIL.		2	2.6		NA	NA
NOT TARGET		35	46.1		75	74.3

* *See next page for explanation of variables.*

TABLE 5-3 *CONTINUED*

AREA	JOBS SUBJECTS			NON-JOBS SUBJECTS		
	N	TARGET GROUP	%	N	TARGET GROUP	%
TOTAL	5,537	3,998	72.2	5,848	2,610	44.6
SOUTHEAST	1,641	1,090	66.4	1,044	372	35.6
36/60 Mos.		824	50.2		274	26.3
AGE, No H.S.		249	15.2		98	9.4
LOSE ELIGIBIL.		17	1.0		NA	NA
NOT TARGET		551	33.6		672	64.4

* VARIABLES
36/60 MOS = On AFDC 36 out of the last 60 months.
Age, No H.S. = Under 24, has not completed high school.
Lose Eligibil. = Will leave AFDC within two years because youngest child turns 18.
Not Target = Not a member of a target group.

NOTE: Data may contain missing observations. Data are rounded. Data are not available for non-JOBS subjects who are about to time out of the system because of the age of their youngest child. See note no. 10.
SOURCE: Missouri Department of Social Services, Research and Evaluation, JOBS Research Data Set.

viduals to the non-target group individuals in both the JOBS and non-JOBS samples. We obtained a Chi-square value of 887.985, which indicates this relationship is statistically significant at Alpha = .001. (See appendix C.) JOBS staff felt this high proportion of target group participants results from the emphasis placed on serving target group individuals by the JOBS state office policy section. Field staff have been instructed to give priority to target group individuals over non-target individuals who volunteer for the JOBS program. Only northeast Missouri failed to achieve the federal mandate of devoting 55 percent of their resources to target group individuals by serving just 54 percent.

National data indicate that all fifty states appear to be serving individuals identified as "most needy." A recent report by the U.S. General Accounting Office (GAO), *Welfare to Work: States Serve Least Job-Ready While Meeting JOBS Participation Rates*, indicates that all states met their mandate to spend 55 percent of their JOBS resources on target group individuals. According to the GAO:

> For fiscal year 1991, concerns that JOBS participation-rate requirements may be discouraging states from serving the least job-ready AFDC recipients, including providing them education and training, are not supported by our review of data states report to HHS. As reported by HHS, all but one state met the 7 percent participation rate for fiscal year 1991 and all spent at least 55 percent of their JOBS budgets on target group members. Of those AFDC recipients served by states in JOBS during this period, 62 percent were target group members.[11]

According to the GAO report, Missouri ranked twenty-first among all states by serving 65 percent target group individuals. Oklahoma ranked first, serving 89 percent target group individuals, while Arizona ranked last, serving 33 percent target group individuals.[12]

AFDC CHARACTERISTIC DATA— JOBS PARTICIPANT PROFILE

To explore the second research question—Are JOBS participants representative of the AFDC population?—we again analyzed the eight key individual characteristics selected by the JOBS staff from the list of available data elements for analysis. Tables 5-4 through 5-13 compare the characteristics of the JOBS subjects with those of the non-JOBS subjects at the state, region, and county levels. The difference in the variances of each characteristic was tested for statistical significance using either analysis of variance (ANOVA) or frequency tables with the Chi-square test.

Again, the characteristics chosen for analysis were age, educational level, work experience, age at birth of first child, length of time on AFDC, number of children, race, and sex. (See appendix A for a definition of the variables used in this chapter. The eight variables are noted by an *.) When combined with receiving welfare, these characteristics theoretically will provide an indication of potential AFDC dependency and the barriers that limit access to the labor market.

Analysis of the age variable reveals that JOBS subjects tend to be younger than non-JOBS subjects. As table 5-4 indicates, the average age of JOBS participants is 24.66 while non-JOBS subjects average 27.96 years of age. Using ANOVA, we find the difference in the mean age is significant, at Alpha = .05, for all subjects and for the subjects in each of the four regions. The age difference was not statistically significant, however, in five of the ten counties.[13]

Examination of educational levels reveals that, overall, JOBS participants tend to have completed slightly more school than non-JOBS

TABLE 5-4

MEAN AGE OF JOBS AND NON-JOBS SUBJECTS

AREA	JOBS SUBJECTS		NON-JOBS SUBJECTS		SIGNIFICANT ALPHA=.05
	N	MEAN	N	MEAN	
TOTAL	5,928	24.66	5,544	27.96	YES
ST. LOUIS	3,087	23.87	2,491	27.37	YES
KANSAS CITY	958	24.81	2,001	28.17	YES
NORTHEAST	82	27.15	90	29.93	YES
LINCOLN	46	27.54	52	29.25	NO
PIKE	36	26.64	38	30.87	YES
SOUTHEAST	1,801	25.84	962	28.91	YES
BUTLER	287	25.81	132	29.87	YES
CAPE GIRARD.	136	26.02	107	27.44	NO
DUNKLIN	403	25.70	159	29.52	YES
MISSISSIPPI	110	27.28	104	27.75	NO
NEW MADRID	298	26.78	84	28.86	NO
PEMISCOT	209	24.12	159	30.03	YES
SCOTT	225	24.92	126	27.98	YES
STODDARD	135	27.12	91	28.93	NO

NOTE: County data may contain missing observations. Data are rounded.
SOURCE: Missouri Department of Social Services, Research and Evaluation, JOBS Research Data Set.

subjects. As table 5-5 indicates, the average number of grades completed for all JOBS subjects is 11.18 while the average for all non-JOBS subjects is 11.09 grades. Using ANOVA, we found the difference in mean educational level is statistically significant, at Alpha =.05, for the total sample and for the St. Louis and southeast regions. The differences, however, were not statistically significant in six of the ten counties. It should also be noted that JOBS staff indicated educational testing of AFDC participants often reveals they function two to three grades below the highest grade they claim to have completed.[14]

TABLE 5-5

MEAN EDUCATIONAL LEVEL OF JOBS AND NON-JOBS SUBJECTS

AREA	JOBS SUBJECTS		NON-JOBS SUBJECTS		SIGNIFICANT ALPHA=.05
	N	MEAN	N	MEAN	
TOTAL	5,723	11.18	5,334	11.09	YES
ST. LOUIS	3,036	11.25	2,419	11.06	YES
KANSAS CITY	943	11.43	1,928	11.39	NO
NORTHEAST	78	11.26	82	11.22	NO
LINCOLN	44	11.14	51	11.20	NO
PIKE	34	11.41	31	11.26	NO
SOUTHEAST	1,666	10.92	905	10.52	YES
BUTLER	247	11.26	120	10.58	YES
CAPE GIRARD.	135	11.89	101	10.91	YES
DUNKLIN	356	10.59	150	10.11	YES
MISSISSIPPI	102	10.84	102	10.61	NO
NEW MADRID	288	10.52	81	10.27	NO
PEMISCOT	200	10.83	147	10.25	YES
SCOTT	216	11.13	122	10.96	NO
STODDARD	122	10.86	82	10.68	NO

NOTE: County data may contain missing observations. Data are rounded.
SOURCE: Missouri Department of Social Services, Research and Evaluation, JOBS Research Data Set.

As table 5-6 indicates, JOBS participants worked slightly less than non-JOBS subjects. JOBS participants worked an average 2.48 months in a twelve-month period compared to 2.92 months for non-JOBS participants. This difference was statistically significant at Alpha = .05. At the regional level, differences in work experience were statistically significant in only one of the four regions, Kansas City, while differences in mean work experience were not statistically significant in any of the counties. In four out of the ten counties, however, JOBS participants had a higher mean work experience than non-JOBS subjects.

TABLE 5-6

MEAN WORK EXPERIENCE DURING THE PREVIOUS TWELVE MONTHS

AREA	JOBS SUBJECTS		NON-JOBS SUBJECTS		SIGNIFICANT ALPHA=.05
	N	MEAN	N	MEAN	
TOTAL	5,914	2.48	5,409	2.92	YES
ST. LOUIS	3,079	2.40	2,439	2.50	NO
KANSAS CITY	954	2.81	1,946	3.56	YES
NORTHEAST	82	3.06	87	3.70	NO
LINCOLN	46	2.72	52	4.12	NO
PIKE	36	3.50	35	3.09	NO
SOUTHEAST	1,799	2.40	937	2.59	NO
BUTLER	287	2.26	129	2.51	NO
CAPE GIRARD.	136	4.10	105	3.62	NO
DUNKLIN	402	2.08	154	2.26	NO
MISSISSIPPI	109	2.71	103	2.43	NO
NEW MADRID	299	2.00	81	2.83	NO
PEMISCOT	209	1.87	125	3.10	NO
SCOTT	225	2.81	153	2.16	NO
STODDARD	132	2.67	87	2.08	NO

NOTE: County data may contain missing observations. Data are rounded.
SOURCE: Missouri Department of Social Services, Research and Evaluation, JOBS Research Data Set.

Overall, JOBS participants had their first child at a younger age than non-JOBS individuals, at a mean age of 19.73 compared to 21.43 years for non-JOBS participants. As indicated in table 5-7, this relationship of earlier child bearing was observed in all ten counties, and was statistically significant in three out of the four regions. Only in northeast Missouri was the mother's age at first birth not statistically significant at Alpha = .05.

JOBS participants, according to table 5-8, have a longer average length of stay on AFDC than do non-JOBS participants. The length of the

TABLE 5-7

MEAN AGE OF AFDC RECIPIENT AT THE BIRTH OF THE FIRST CHILD

AREA	JOBS SUBJECTS		NON-JOBS SUBJECTS		SIGNIFICANT ALPHA=.05
	N	MEAN	N	MEAN	
TOTAL	5,730	19.73	5,445	21.42	YES
ST. LOUIS	2,973	19.43	2,436	21.14	YES
KANSAS CITY	925	19.87	1,970	21.53	YES
NORTHEAST	80	20.88	91	21.97	NO
LINCOLN	44	20.82	53	22.30	NO
PIKE	36	20.94	38	21.50	NO
SOUTHEAST	1,752	20.13	948	21.89	YES
BUTLER	282	20.01	138	22.18	YES
CAPE GIRARD.	135	21.44	111	22.01	NO
DUNKLIN	389	19.80	161	22.56	YES
MISSISSIPPI	107	20.48	99	20.76	NO
NEW MADRID	289	20.47	77	20.73	NO
PEMISCOT	203	19.33	145	22.23	YES
SCOTT	217	19.96	125	21.25	YES
STODDARD	130	20.46	92	21.95	YES

NOTE: County data may contain missing observations. Data are rounded.
SOURCE: Missouri Department of Social Services, Research and Evaluation, JOBS Research Data Set.

most current AFDC spell is 32.79 months for JOBS participants while only 29.56 months for non-JOBS subjects. In only one county, Mississippi, did non-JOBS individuals experience a shorter length of time on AFDC than JOBS participants. As table 5-8 indicates, the difference in the mean length of stay on AFDC was statistically significant in three out of four regions, and in one out of the ten counties.

JOBS participants have slightly more children than non-JOBS subjects. According to table 5-9, JOBS participants have an average of 2.2 children while non-JOBS individuals have 2.1 children. This difference

TABLE 5-8

MEAN LENGTH OF STAY ON AFDC (MONTHS)

AREA	JOBS SUBJECTS		NON-JOBS SUBJECTS		SIGNIFICANT ALPHA=.05
	N	MEAN	N	MEAN	
TOTAL	5,750	32.79	5,342	29.56	YES
ST. LOUIS	2,996	35.37	2,415	36.72	NO
KANSAS CITY	920	25.90	1,914	22.54	YES
NORTHEAST	80	22.06	89	14.98	YES
LINCOLN	45	22.04	51	13.51	NO
PIKE	35	22.09	38	16.95	NO
SOUTHEAST	1,754	32.49	924	26.76	YES
BUTLER	281	28.17	128	24.38	NO
CAPE GIRARD.	127	28.53	106	20.72	NO
DUNKLIN	396	26.72	151	24.03	NO
MISSISSIPPI	109	31.11	100	32.81	NO
NEW MADRID	291	43.50	81	31.54	NO
PEMISCOT	200	41.55	151	30.41	YES
SCOTT	217	31.00	118	29.10	NO
STODDARD	133	28.41	89	21.61	NO

NOTE: County data may contain missing observations. Data are rounded.
SOURCE: Missouri Department of Social Services, Research and Evaluation, JOBS Research Data Set.

is statistically significant at Alpha =.05, as are the differences in the Kansas City and southeast regions. At the county level, this difference was not statistically significant.

Analysis of the race variable indicates JOBS participants tend to include slightly higher minority group representation than the sample of non-JOBS subjects. According to table 5-10, 3,982 individuals, or 67.01 percent of all JOBS participants, were coded as minority group members compared to 3,886 individuals, or 66.4 percent, for the non-JOBS group. While the difference appears small, controlling for area, Chi-square indi-

TABLE 5-9

MEAN NUMBER OF CHILDREN IN THE FAMILY

AREA	JOBS SUBJECTS		NON-JOBS SUBJECTS		SIGNIFICANT ALPHA=.05
	N	MEAN	N	MEAN	
TOTAL	5,934	2.20	5,845	2.10	YES
ST. LOUIS	3,091	2.23	2,577	2.21	NO
KANSAS CITY	959	2.26	2,124	2.00	YES
NORTHEAST	82	2.22	101	2.06	NO
LINCOLN	46	2.20	59	2.07	NO
PIKE	36	2.25	42	2.05	NO
SOUTHEAST	1,802	2.12	1,043	2.01	YES
BUTLER	288	2.02	150	2.01	NO
CAPE GIRARD.	136	1.82	131	1.87	NO
DUNKLIN	402	2.18	178	2.00	NO
MISSISSIPPI	110	2.05	104	1.98	NO
NEW MADRID	299	2.17	84	1.88	NO
PEMISCOT	209	2.47	163	2.19	NO
SCOTT	225	2.06	132	2.14	NO
STODDARD	133	1.90	101	1.89	NO

NOTE: County data may contain missing observations. Data are rounded.
SOURCE: Missouri Department of Social Services, Research and Evaluation, JOBS Research Data Set.

TABLE 5-10

RACE OF AFDC RECIPIENTS

AREA	JOBS SUBJECTS		NON-JOBS SUBJECTS		SIGNIFICANT ALPHA=.05
	N	%	N	%	
TOTAL	5,935		5,848		YES
WHITE	1,953	32.9	1,962	33.6	
BLACK	3,937	66.3	3,769	64.5	
OTHER	45	.8	117	1.9	
ST. LOUIS	3,091		2,579		YES
WHITE	306	9.9	402	15.6	
BLACK	2,775	89.8	2,148	83.3	
OTHER	10	.3	29	1.1	
KANSAS CITY	959		2,124		YES
WHITE	263	27.4	721	34.0	
BLACK	667	69.6	1,322	62.2	
OTHER	29	3.0	79	3.8	
NORTHEAST	82		101		NO
WHITE	70	85.4	93	92.1	
BLACK	11	13.4	8	7.9	
OTHER	1	1.2	0		
SOUTHEAST	1,803		1,044		NO
WHITE	1,310	72.9	746	71.5	
BLACK	484	26.8	291	27.9	
OTHER	5	.3	7	.6	

SOURCE: Missouri Department of Social Services, Research and Evaluation, JOBS Research Data Set.

cated that the difference in the race variable between the JOBS and the non-JOBS groups was statistically significant at Alpha =.05. The difference was also statistically significant in two of the four regions, St. Louis and Kansas City. At the county level, the difference in the race variable was statistically significant in three of the ten counties.

Analysis of the sex variable, table 5-11, indicates women are slightly more represented in the JOBS participant group than in the comparison group. While 94.5 percent of the sample of non-JOBS AFDC recipients

TABLE 5-11

SEX OF AFDC RECIPIENTS

AREA	JOBS SUBJECTS		NON-JOBS SUBJECTS		SIGNIFICANT ALPHA=.05
	N	%	N	%	
TOTAL	5,935		5,848		YES
FEMALE	5,789	97.5	5,528	94.5	
MALE	146	2.5	320	5.5	
ST. LOUIS	3,091		2,579		YES
FEMALE	3,049	98.6	2,485	96.4	
MALE	42	1.4	94	3.6	
KANSAS CITY	959		2,124		YES
FEMALE	937	97.7	1,980	93.2	
MALE	22	2.3	144	6.8	
NORTHEAST	82		101		NO
FEMALE	76	92.7	94	93.1	
MALE	6	7.3	7	6.9	
SOUTHEAST	1,803		1,044		YES
FEMALE	1,727	95.8	969	92.8	
MALE	76	4.2	75	7.2	

SOURCE: Missouri Department of Social Services, Research and Evaluation, JOBS Research Data Set.

were women, 97.5 percent of the JOBS participants were women. Controlling for area, Chi-square indicated this relationship was statistically significant at Alpha = .05. In addition, three of the four regions exhibited the same pattern, with northeast Missouri being the exception to the trend. Also, the difference in the sex variable was statistically significant in three of the four regions. Again, northeast Missouri was the exception. At the county level, the increased number of women participating in the JOBS group was statistically significant in three out of ten counties.

As table 5-12 indicates, the difference in the means of all eight demographic characteristics was statistically significant when all JOBS subjects were compared to all non-JOBS subjects. Regional and county-level data, however, did not exhibit the same consistent trend. In Kansas City, the differences in seven of the eight variables were statistically significant as were six in the southeast region, five in St. Louis, and only two in northeast Missouri.

County-level data varied considerably. In two counties, Lincoln and New Madrid, none of the eight characteristics were statistically significant, while six of the characteristics were statistically significant in Pemiscot County. One characteristic was statistically significant in Cape Girardeau, Mississippi, Pike, and Stoddard counties; two in Scott County; and four in Butler and Dunklin counties.

The age characteristic was statistically significant in the most locations, four regions and five counties, followed closely by AFDC recipients' age at time of first birth, which was statistically significant in three regions and five counties. The work-experience and number-of-children characteristics were significant in the least number of locations, with work experience being statistically significant only in Kansas City and number of children statistically significant only in Kansas City and the southeast areas.

Comparing the JOBS population to the non-JOBS subjects, JOBS participants tend to be younger, have slightly more education, have worked less in the previous twelve months, started having children at a slightly younger age and have slightly more children, have been on AFDC a little longer, are more likely to be a member of a minority group, and are more likely to be women than non-JOBS participants. And while these differences are statistically significant, as table 5-13 indicates, the differences in many of the characteristics are relatively minor.

FINDINGS

With regard to the first research question, we find evidence to support the contention that the Missouri JOBS program is providing services to the "potentially long-term dependent" and is not "creaming" participants. As data on tables 5-2 and 5-3 indicate, the JOBS participants possess attributes that are perceived as more unfavorable than the non-JOBS

TABLE 5-12

SIGNIFICANCE OF KEY DEMOGRAPHIC CHARACTERISTICS BY AREA

	\multicolumn{8}{c}{YES = Significant at Alpha .05 Variable*}	TOTAL SIGNIF. VAR.
	1	2	3	4	5	6	7	8	
TOTAL	YES	YES	YES	YES	YES	YES	YES	YES	8
ST. LOUIS	YES	YES	NO	YES	NO	NO	YES	YES	5
KANSAS CITY	YES	NO	YES	YES	YES	YES	YES	YES	7
NORTHEAST	YES	NO	NO	NO	YES	NO	NO	NO	2
LINCOLN	NO	NO	NO	NO	NO	NO	NO	NO	0
PIKE	YES	NO	NO	NO	NO	NO	NO	NO	1
SOUTHEAST	YES	YES	NO	YES	YES	YES	NO	YES	6
BUTLER	YES	YES	NO	YES	NO	NO	NO	YES	4
CAPE GIRARD.	NO	YES	NO	NO	NO	NO	NO	NO	1
DUNKLIN	YES	YES	NO	YES	NO	NO	YES	NO	4
MISSISSIPPI	NO	NO	NO	NO	NO	NO	YES	NO	1
NEW MADRID	NO	NO	NO	NO	NO	NO	NO	NO	0
PEMISCOT	YES	YES	NO	YES	YES	NO	YES	YES	6
SCOTT	YES	NO	NO	YES	NO	NO	NO	NO	2
STODDARD	NO	NO	NO	YES	NO	NO	NO	NO	1
TOTAL YES	10	7	2	9	5	3	6	6	48

* 1=Age   2=Education   3=Work Experience   4=Age at Birth of First Child
5=Length of Stay on AFDC   6=Number of Children   7=Race   8=Sex

subjects. Therefore, we reject hypothesis 1, that the most dependent individuals are not receiving JOBS services. Similarly, we also reject hypothesis 2 that the percent of target group individuals in JOBS is less than the percent of target group individuals represented in the general AFDC population. A Chi-square test of significance indicates the differences between the two groups is statistically significant.

With regard to the second research question, we find that JOBS participants are different from the AFDC non-JOBS population, at least statistically. The differences for all eight individual characteristics selected for analysis were statistically significant at Alpha = .05, even though many of the differences were relatively minor. *We cannot, however, accept many of the statistically significant differences as substantive.* It is difficult to argue that the differences noted on table 5-13 between the JOBS and non-JOBS subjects, when analyzed individually, support the contention that JOBS subjects are substantially different from non-JOBS

TABLE 5-13

COMPARISON OF MEANS FOR EIGHT KEY VARIABLES
JOBS SUBJECTS AND NON-JOBS SUBJECTS

AREA	JOBS SUBJECTS		NON-JOBS SUBJECTS		DIFF. (+/-)
	N	MEAN	N	MEAN	
TOTAL	5,935		5,848		YES
AGE	5,928	24.66	5,544	27.96	-3.30 YRS
EDUCATION	5,723	11.18	5,334	11.09	+0.09 YRS
WORK EXP.	5,914	2.48	5,409	2.92	-0.44 MOS
AGE/FIRST BIRTH	5,730	19.73	5,445	21.42	-1.69 YRS
TIME ON AFDC	5,750	32.79	5,342	29.56	+3.23 MOS
NO. CHILDREN	5,934	2.20	5,845	2.10	+0.10 CHILD
MINORITY %	5,935	67.1%	5,848	66.4%	+0.70 %
WOMEN %	5,935	97.5%	5,529	94.5%	+3.00 %

SOURCE: Missouri Department of Social Services, Research and Evaluation, JOBS Research Data Set.

subjects. What can be argued, however, is that when the eight individual attributes are analyzed in aggregate, the JOBS subjects possess characteristics which are consistently slightly more "unfavorable." These characteristics are potentially associated with dependency or they serve as a barrier to labor force participation. We reject hypothesis 3 that there is no statistically significant difference between the characteristics of JOBS participants and those of AFDC recipients who did not participate in JOBS.

To further support the above findings, we identified one other factor inherent in Missouri's JOBS implementation process that may have contributed to reduced "creaming" of program participants. During the first year, JOBS staff were required to meet a federal mandate to enroll 7 percent of the state's eligible AFDC recipients in the JOBS program or lose federal JOBS matching funds. (See chapter 4.) This federal participation requirement increased to 11 percent during the second year.

On several occasions, JOBS field staff indicated they were under considerable pressure from the state office to meet caseload participation standards as quickly as possible. The case managers felt the pressure from Jefferson City affected their discretion about which AFDC clients entered the JOBS program. Staff repeatedly indicated they could not be as selective as they liked since they felt they were being forced to bring everyone who volunteered into JOBS. They indicated that a number of the people who entered JOBS during the first two years had problems that the program could not address effectively and that the pressure to enroll participants quickly may have negatively impacted the early effectiveness of JOBS. It is likely this situation resulted in less "creaming" of participants since it inhibited field staff from enrolling participants perceived as "more favorable" at the expense of people who may been viewed as a bad risk.

NOTES

1. JOBS participant from Scott County, Missouri, confidential interview with author, 29 October 1992.

2. Nancy Dickinson, "Which Welfare Strategies Work?" *Social Work* 31 (July/August 1986): 267–268.

3. JOBS subjects, the experimental group, all volunteered to participate in JOBS after attending a program orientation. The Missouri JOBS program has not called in mandatory participants because it has sufficient volunteers.

4. Greg Duncan and Saul Hoffman, "The Use and Effects of Welfare: A Survey of Recent Evidence," paper presented at the conference on The Political Economy of the Transfer Society, Tallahassee, Florida (November 1987), 3–7; also, Irwin Garfinkel and Sara S. McLanahan, *Single Mothers and Their Children: A New American Dilemma?* (Washington, D.C.); Mary Jo Bane and David Ellwood, "The Dynamics of Dependence and the Routes to Self-Sufficiency," final report to the Department of Health and Human Services (Cambridge, MA: Harvard University, Kennedy School of Government, 1983), and their other work "Slipping Into and Out of Poverty: The Dynamics of Spells," *The Journal of Human Resources* (1986).

5. Greg Duncan and Saul Hoffman, "The Use and Effects of Welfare: A Survey of Recent Evidence," paper presented at the conference on The Political Economy of the Transfer Society, Tallahassee, Florida (November 1987).

6. State of Missouri, Governor's Interagency Working Group on Adolescent Pregnancy, *Two Generations at Risk*, Jefferson City, Missouri (January 1987), 20–23.

7. Wayne Schramm, Research Analyst IV, Missouri Department of Health, State Center For Health Statistics, unpublished data from analysis of first births in Missouri, interview with author, 18 February 1993.

8. Greg Duncan and Saul Hoffman, "The Use and Effects of Welfare: A Survey of Recent Evidence."

9. JOBS staff from the Southeast Region, Division of Family Services Area III, confidential interview with author, 28–29 October 1992.

10. Data are not available for the JOBS target individuals who are receiving AFDC and are not in JOBS and who will lose AFDC eligibility within two years because their youngest child will be eighteen years of age. Due to our oversight, these data elements were not requested from

the Department of Social Services when the JOBS Research Data Set was originally compiled; however, Department of Social Services' research and evaluation staff estimate that less than 1 percent of non-JOBS subjects will fall into this category. It should also be noted that there is no double-counting between the three target group categories. Target group individuals are counted only once and are prioritized by category. It is possible, however, that an individual may belong to more than one target group.

11.   U. S. General Accounting Office, *Welfare to Work: States Serve Least Job-Ready While Meeting JOBS Participation Rates* (Washington, D.C., November 1992), 2. Also, it is possible for states to serve less than 55 percent target group individuals while spending 55 percent of their resources on target group participants. States can do this by enrolling target group individuals in the more expensive JOBS components such as higher education and vocational training as opposed to job search.

12.   The U. S. General Accounting Office report *Welfare to Work: States Serve Least Job Ready While Meeting JOBS Participation Rates* indicates Missouri served 65 percent target group individuals versus 72.2 percent reported on table 5–12. The difference can be attributed to the differences in time periods and geographic coverage. The GAO report includes all JOBS participants for FY 1991. This study is for selected counties and includes both FY 1991 and 1992. The GAO and Department of Health and Human Services do not collect data concerning the number of target group individuals in the general AFDC population.

13.   While many of the variables selected for analysis were statistically significant, we can not accept most of the differences in the variables' descriptive statistics as substantive. Refer to chapter 5, "AFDC Characteristic Data—Who is Being Served by JOBS," for an indication of the substantive significance of each variable.

14.   Donald Holt, FUTURES (JOBS) Program Manager for Eastern Missouri, Missouri Department of Social Services, Division of Family Services, interview with author, 5 February 1993.

VI

Job Opportunities and Basic Skills Training Program: Are the Participants Better Off? Are the Taxpayers Better Off?

My name is Traci. I am twenty-six years old and the mother of a four-year-old. In 1986, I married a man who is an alcoholic and a drug addict. This was your typical abusive marriage. In 1989, my daughter and I left. I worked at various dead-end jobs. I have been on and off AFDC for the past three and one-half years.

In January 1990, I started college. While in school, I also had to work full-time. In April 1990, I had to quit school because I could no longer afford to pay a baby-sitter sixteen hours per day. I was very depressed and down on myself. I felt I would never be able to provide my daughter with a good life.

In September 1991, I decided to try school again. This time I enrolled at Four Rivers Area Vo-Tech in nursing. The major difference this time was the FU-TURES Program. This was an extremely difficult school. It required at least three hours of homework every night. Needless to say, there were times when I became discouraged and I wanted to quit, but I knew if I wanted to give my daughter a better life, I had to stick it out.

It all eventually paid off. On August 14, 1992, I graduated from nursing school. This was one of the happiest days of my life. I had finally made it. This was the first thing I had ever completed. I started working August 19, 1992. I will be making enough money to provide my daughter with a good life. I will not have to be on AFDC any longer. For the first time, I know what it really means to be independent.

I truly feel I would not have made it if not for the FUTURES program. To all of you just starting school, remember why you have chosen to go to school. There will be times when you want to quit, but keep your goal in mind. When it is all over, you see that all the hard work was worth it.

—Letter from a Missouri
FUTURES participant[1]

In state fiscal years 1991 and 1992, the Missouri JOBS program spent approximately $12.1 million helping people like Traci reduce their dependency on the public welfare system. In addition, another $15.6 million was expended for child care over the same time period to help AFDC recipients, including JOBS participants, take part in education, training, and job-search activities.[2] In this chapter, we examine the program outcomes associated with Missouri JOBS participation, contrasting the experiences of the JOBS participants with those of non-JOBS subjects.

RESEARCH QUESTIONS

The central question for any evaluative study of the outcome phase of the public policy process is: Are the outcomes derived from a specific public policy the desired ones? Since the stated purpose of the Job Opportunities and Basic Skills Training Program (JOBS) is to reduce welfare dependency, the corresponding question is: Are the people who participate in JOBS less dependent on the public welfare system than people who do not participate in JOBS?

Chapter 6 will focus on analysis of the key outcome data contained in the Division of Family Services (DFS) JOBS Research Data Set. Specifically, chapter 6 addresses the following research questions and tests their related hypotheses to determine if the JOBS program is realizing benefits in excess of program costs.

Research Question 3: Does JOBS participation result in increased labor force participation and decreased public assistance utilization?
• Hypothesis 4: There is no significant difference between the labor force participation of JOBS subjects and that of non-JOBS subjects.
• Hypothesis 5: There is no significant difference between the AFDC grant amount received by JOBS subjects and that received by non-JOBS subjects.

Research Question 4: Which JOBS activities have the most impact on reduced AFDC dependency?
• Hypothesis 6: Participation in a specific JOBS activity component will not affect JOBS participation outcomes such as increased labor force participation and reduced AFDC utilization.

Research Question 5: Are the people who successfully complete JOBS and enter employment different from the individuals who participate in JOBS and do not enter employment?
• Hypothesis 7: There is no significant difference between the characteristics of individuals who complete JOBS training and those who participate, but do not complete training.

Research Question 6: Is JOBS cost-effective?
• Hypothesis 8: In its early stages, JOBS is not cost-effective.

Research Question 7: Is there a significant difference in JOBS program outcomes for different geographic areas of Missouri?
• Hypothesis 9: There are no significant regional differences in program outcomes—labor force participation and AFDC grant amounts.

RESEARCH OVERVIEW

We investigated research question 3 by focusing on two variables contained in the DFS JOBS Research Data Set—quarterly earnings and current AFDC grant amount. The total earnings and the most recent AFDC grants to JOBS and non-JOBS subjects were compared and analyzed for differences. Theoretically, both variables provide an indication of an individual's degree of welfare dependency since the less an individual works, the greater is her or his dependency on the public welfare system. In addition, when AFDC recipients earn wages, their AFDC grants are reduced according to a formula which eventually taxes labor market income 100 percent—that is, for every dollar an individual earns, they lose a dollar in AFDC benefits. Therefore, reduced AFDC grants provide an indication of "less need" and less dependency.[3]

Before proceeding with the analysis of the two dependency indicators, a note of caution is necessary. While earnings and AFDC benefits are the traditional hard indicators of dependency, using these indicators has some limitations. For instance, in the early stages of an employment and training program, individuals who are seriously pursuing educational activities may reduce their labor market participation until they complete their education.

This phenomenon is analogous to the situation of two individuals who graduate from high school; one goes to work immediately while the other goes to college. If earnings are considered to be the only measure of success, the individual who is working would be perceived as more successful than the individual in school, at least in the initial four- to five-year period. Eventually, however, we would expect to see the individual with more education have higher earnings in addition to other benefits such as a higher degree of job stability, higher potential for advancement, a higher skill level, and greater opportunity to learn new skills.

QUARTERLY WAGE DATA

Comparison of the wages earned by JOBS participants with those of non-JOBS subjects indicates that in all regions and counties JOBS participants earned less than non-JOBS subjects. For all study subjects, the JOBS group earned an average of $2,253 in the twenty-four month period, July 1, 1990, through June 30, 1992, compared to $4,685 for the non-JOBS group, which was comprised of a random sample of AFDC recipients who did not participate in JOBS. Analysis of Variance (ANOVA) indicates this earnings pattern is statistically significant in all regions and in five of the ten counties. (See table 6-1.)

Table 6-1 indicates that JOBS participation has a negative impact on an individual's earnings at first. This is not surprising given the educational needs of many women in the program. The JOBS program has only been operating for two years in the St. Louis and southeast regions and for one year in the Kansas City and northeast regions. Many participants are still completing remedial courses; others are enrolled in longer-term study programs such as nursing or college, so their earnings are temporarily reduced.

Tables 6-2 and 6-3 examine earnings from different perspectives. In table 6-2, the total earnings of the 632 individuals who have completed

TABLE 6-1

AVERAGE TOTAL EARNINGS OF JOBS AND NON-JOBS SUBJECTS, JULY 1, 1990, THROUGH JUNE 30, 1992

AREA	JOBS SUBJECTS		NON-JOBS SUBJECTS		SIGNIFICANT ALPHA=.05
	N	MEAN ($)	N	MEAN ($)	
TOTAL	5,935	2,253	5,848	4,685	YES
St. Louis	3,091	2,424	2,579	4,412	YES
Kansas City	959	2,138	2,124	5,629	YES
Northeast	82	2,818	101	6,116	YES
Lincoln	46	2,625	59	7,062	YES
Pike	36	3,065	42	4,783	NO
Southeast	1,803	1,994	1,044	3,302	YES
Butler	288	2,183	150	3,265	YES
Cape Girardeau	136	3,242	132	4,820	YES
Dunklin	403	1,563	178	2,909	YES
Mississippi	110	1,765	104	2,851	NO
New Madrid	299	1,413	84	3,830	YES
Pemiscot	209	1,615	163	2,569	NO
Scott	225	2,499	132	3,050	NO
Stoddard	133	2,853	101	3,604	NO

NOTE: Data may contain missing observations. Data are rounded.
SOURCE: Missouri Department of Social Services, Research and Evaluation, JOBS Research Data Set.

the JOBS program so far are compared to the total earnings of 5,848 non-JOBS participants by region, for the same time period. The earnings of JOBS participants in all regions except northeast Missouri were less than those of their non-JOBS counterparts during the quarters the program has been in operation. Again all differences in earnings are significant at Alpha = .05 except for northeast Missouri. It will be interesting to collect further data for this income comparison as the program progresses; if JOBS is having its intended effect, we anticipate that the earnings of those who complete JOBS will overtake and surpass the earnings of people not involved in the JOBS program.[4]

Table 6-3 supports these projections. This table compares the earnings of individuals who completed JOBS with the earnings of the total JOBS population. Individuals who completed JOBS had an average total eight-quarter earnings increase of $545 over the total JOBS population. The increases varied from a low of $214 in the southeast region to a high of $6,146 in the northeast region, with participants gaining $1,124 in Kansas City, and St. Louis residents gaining $545 in total wages.

Although the total earnings variable may not be an entirely valid indicator of the increased earnings potential derived from JOBS partici-

TABLE 6-2

TOTAL EARNINGS OF JOBS (COMPLETED) AND NON-JOBS SUBJECTS, JULY 1, 1990, THROUGH JUNE 30, 1992

AREA	JOBS SUBJECTS (COMPLETED)		NON-JOBS SUBJECTS		SIGNIFICANT ALPHA=.05
	N	MEAN ($)	N	MEAN ($)	
TOTAL	632	2,798	5,848	4,685	YES
St. Louis	315	2,968	2,579	4,412	YES
Kansas City	88	3,262	2,124	5,629	YES
Northeast	6	8,958	101	6,116	NO
Southeast	223	2,208	1,044	3,302	YES

NOTE: Data may contain missing observations. Data are rounded.
SOURCE: Missouri Department of Social Services, Research and Evaluation, JOBS Research Data Set.

TABLE 6-3

TOTAL EARNINGS OF JOBS (COMPLETED) AND ALL JOBS SUBJECTS,
JULY 1, 1990, THROUGH JUNE 30, 1992

AREA	JOBS SUBJECTS (COMPLETED)		JOBS SUBJECTS (TOTAL)		DIFFERENCE (+OR-)
	N	MEAN ($)	N	MEAN ($)	($)
TOTAL	632	2,798	5,935	2,253	+ 545
St. Louis	315	2,968	3,091	2,424	+ 544
Kansas City	88	3,262	959	2,138	+1,124
Northeast	6	8,958	82	2,818	+6,140
Southeast	223	2,208	1,803	1,994	+ 214

NOTE: Data may contain missing observations. Data are rounded.
SOURCE: Missouri Department of Social Services, Research and Evaluation, JOBS Research Data Set.

pation, it seems to correlate positively with program participation. Theoretically, the total earnings variable is influenced by wage quarters where the JOBS participant is voluntarily out of the labor force because of a commitment to education or training. Table 6-4 examines the average quarterly earnings of JOBS and non-JOBS subjects for each of the eight quarters. If JOBS is having a positive impact on earnings, we would expect to see quarterly earnings of JOBS participants increase as the JOBS program matures and people complete training.

This expectation is substantiated by the JOBS data presently available. Table 6-4 shows that the earnings of JOBS subjects who completed program activities increased substantially in the last quarter. According to table 6-4, average quarterly earnings for the non-JOBS group were stable over the eight-quarter period between July 1, 1990, and June 30, 1992, ranging from $557 to $613. For the JOBS group, earnings reached a low of $221 in the third quarter of 1991, down from third quarter 1990 earnings of $448. This drop supports the staff's observation that individuals reduce their work hours to participate in JOBS components. Earning rebounded, however, to $668 by the second quarter of 1992—which is higher than the highest quarter of earning for non-JOBS participants.

TABLE 6-4

AVERAGE QUARTERLY EARNINGS OF ALL JOBS PARTICIPANTS,
JOBS PARTICIPANTS WHO COMPLETED JOBS, JOBS PARTICIPANTS
WHO COMPLETED JOBS AND ARE EMPLOYED, AND NON-JOBS SUBJECTS

	JOBS SUBJECTS (TOTAL) N=5,935	JOBS SUBJECTS (COMPLETED) N=632	JOBS SUBJECTS (COMP/EMP) N=263	NON-JOBS SUBJECTS (TOTAL) N=5,848
QUARTER	($)	($)	($)	($)
1990, 3RD	326	448	565	590
1990, 4TH	297	382	471	613
1991, 1ST	222	268	294	557
1991, 2ND	243	258	370	591
1991, 3RD	250	221	355	580
1991, 4TH	281	235	395	602
1992, 1ST	269	317	607	559
1992, 2ND	364	668	1,269	592

NOTE: Data may contain missing observations, not all subjects included in each quarter's data had wages. Average quarterly earnings listed are for subjects with wages. Data are rounded.
SOURCE: Missouri Department of Social Services, Research and Evaluation, JOBS Research Data Set.

The earnings of this group also surpassed those of the non-JOBS group in the final quarter of this study. Although definitive conclusions cannot be drawn from these data, it does appear JOBS participants have the potential for future long-term improvement and increased self-suffi-ciency due to increased education and job skills.

The experiences of the ex-participants who completed JOBS and who were employed at the time of completion adds additional support to the contention that the Missouri JOBS program is having a positive impact on earnings. As table 6-4 indicates, the eighth-quarter earnings of this group increased to $1,269 from a low point of $294 during the third quarter of this study. This compares to eighth-quarter earnings of $364 for the aggregate JOBS population, $668 for those who completed JOBS, and $592 for the non-JOBS subjects.

AFDC GRANT AMOUNT

The AFDC grant amount is another potential indicator of an individual's dependency on the public welfare system. Generally, the higher the grant amount, the greater the dependency. When a AFDC recipient works and earns income, her or his grant is reduced according to a formula that eventually takes away one dollar for every dollar of income. Therefore, individuals who are working and are less dependent on AFDC would receive lower AFDC grants.[5]

Analysis of the most recent AFDC grant of JOBS and non-JOBS subjects indicates that in all regions and counties the most recent AFDC grant amount is higher for the JOBS population than for the non-JOBS population. Table 6-5 shows that, for all subjects, the JOBS group had an average AFDC grant amount of $246.85 versus $227.22 for non-JOBS subjects. ANOVA indicated this difference was statistically significant at the .05 level as were the differences in grant amounts for all four regions.

Controlling for individuals who have completed JOBS, table 6-6 indicates that the most recent AFDC grants of individuals who have completed JOBS average $15.37 less than the AFDC grants of non-JOBS subjects. Again, ANOVA indicates this difference is discernible at the .05 level. The difference in AFDC grant amounts was also statistically significant in the St. Louis region. While the differences were not statistically significant in the Kansas City, southeast, and northeast regions, individuals who have completed JOBS received lower AFDC grants in two of the three regions than the non-JOBS subjects.

It is likely the AFDC grant variable is influenced by the same factor that influences the earnings variable. That is, if individuals make a commitment to participate in JOBS educational and training activities, they reduce their work efforts so AFDC grants would be expected to be higher for this population than for the population not participating in JOBS. In addition, as tables 6-6 and 6-7 indicate, individuals who complete JOBS tend to have lower AFDC grants than either the total JOBS population or non-JOBS subjects. This indicates that individuals who complete JOBS may be entering the labor market at a salary that reduces their grants, even if their income is not sufficient to remove them at once from the AFDC rolls.

TABLE 6-5

MOST RECENT AVERAGE MONTHLY AFDC GRANT AMOUNTS FOR JOBS AND NON-JOBS SUBJECTS (JULY 1990–JUNE 1992)

AREA	JOBS SUBJECTS		NON-JOBS SUBJECTS		SIGNIFICANT ALPHA=.05
	N	MEAN ($)	N	MEAN ($)	
TOTAL	5,935	246.85	5,848	227.22	YES
St. Louis	3,091	245.33	2,579	237.20	YES
Kansas City	959	263.32	2,124	222.88	YES
Northeast	82	263.62	101	202.40	YES
Lincoln	46	243.11	59	209.63	NO
Pike	36	289.83	42	192.24	YES
Southeast	1,803	239.92	1,044	213.81	YES
Butler	288	221.07	150	193.01	NO
Cape Girardeau	136	206.51	132	176.55	NO
Dunklin	403	261.56	178	210.05	YES
Mississippi	110	249.39	104	232.38	NO
New Madrid	299	255.24	84	238.75	NO
Pemiscot	209	246.45	163	234.13	NO
Scott	225	240.16	132	228.01	NO
Stoddard	133	208.83	101	196.44	NO

NOTE: Data may contain missing observations. Data are rounded.
SOURCE: Missouri Department of Social Services, Research and Evaluation, JOBS Research Data Set.

TABLE 6-6

MOST RECENT MONTHLY AFDC GRANT AMOUNTS FOR JOBS (COMPLETED)
AND NON-JOBS SUBJECTS

| | JOBS SUBJECTS (COMPLETED) | | NON-JOBS SUBJECTS | | DIFF. (±) | SIG. .05 |
	N	MEAN ($)	N	MEAN ($)		
TOTAL	632	211.85	5,848	227.22	-15.37	YES
St. Louis	315	216.92	2,579	237.20	-20.28	YES
Kansas City	88	227.92	2,124	222.88	+ 5.04	NO
Northeast	6	162.00	101	202.40	-40.40	NO
Southeast	223	199.70	1,044	213.81	-14.11	NO

NOTE: Data may contain missing observations. Data are rounded.
SOURCE: Missouri Department of Social Services, Research and Evaluation, JOBS
Research Data Set.

TABLE 6-7

MOST RECENT AVERAGE MONTHLY AFDC GRANT AMOUNTS FOR
ALL JOBS AND JOBS (COMPLETED) SUBJECTS

| | JOBS SUBJECTS (COMPLETED) | | JOBS SUBJECTS (TOTAL) | | DIFF. (±) |
	N	MEAN ($)	N	MEAN ($)	
TOTAL	632	211.85	5,935	246.85	-35.00
St. Louis	315	216.92	3,091	245.33	-28.41
Kansas City	88	227.92	959	263.32	-35.40
Northeast	6	162.00	82	263.62	-101.62
Southeast	223	199.70	1,803	239.92	-40.22

NOTE: Data may contain missing observations. Data are rounded.
SOURCE: Missouri Department of Social Services, Research and Evaluation, JOBS
Research Data Set.

FACTORS CONTRIBUTING TO REDUCED
DEPENDENCY AND INCREASED EARNINGS

To examine which factors have the most impact on reduced welfare dependency, as measured by the dependent variable of total quarterly earnings (research question 4), we used the Statistical Analysis System (SAS) to generate Ordinary Least Squares (OLS) regression statistics for the twenty-one independent variables contained on the JOBS Research Data Set that might potentially influence an individual's earnings and welfare dependency. The regression statistics contain independent variables, which include local economic indicators, participant attributes, and JOBS component activities. These were only generated for research subjects who had participated in JOBS.

Theoretically, local economic conditions affect an individual's ability to obtain employment, thereby contributing to an area's dependency on government assistance and services. If there are no jobs available in an area, or if the jobs available are low-wage/low-stability, it follows that area residents will be more reliant on government assistance than individuals from areas with healthy economies. Factors such as the county unemployment rate, the proportion of the county population living in poverty, or the percent on public assistance provide an indication of local economic well being.

Also, as discussed earlier in chapters 1 and 3, numerous studies have found strong correlations between welfare dependency and individual characteristics. Previously cited research by noted poverty and social policy scholars such as Greg Duncan, Saul Hoffman, Mary Jo Bane, David Ellwood, Irwin Garfinkel, and Sara S. McLanahan indicates that people who have low educational attainment, little work experience, children at an early age, and an established pattern of welfare use are disproportionately represented on the public welfare rolls.[6]

In addition, we would expect access to employment and training services and the type of services available in an area to have a positive impact on the earnings of people who participate in JOBS. Hypothetically, the number of JOBS case managers assigned to a county provides an indication of access to employment and training services. In addition, specific JOBS services, such as job-search assistance, remedial education, and vocational training, are expected to have a positive impact on dependency since theoretically, as individuals' educational and skill levels increase, they should become more competitive and face fewer labor market barriers.

OLS regression was performed on the twenty-one independent variables contained in table 6-8, modeling each with the dependent variable of total earnings. The regression model identified nine independent variables that were significant at Alpha = .05. The most significant variable was work experience followed in order by educational level, the AFDC recipient's age, number of children in the AFDC case, the AFDC recipient's age at the birth of her first child, participation in a high school/GED component, the St. Louis regional indicator, the Kansas City regional indicator, and participation in a job-search/job-readiness component. In addition, another three variables were significant at Alpha = .10. These were JOBS completion, participation in post-secondary education activities, and length of time on AFDC.

The participant's age at the time of the first child's birth, the number of children in the AFDC case, participation in a high school component, participation in post-secondary education, and JOBS participation in Kansas City all had a negative impact on earnings. Previous work experience, educational level, age, JOBS participation in the St. Louis area, participation in a job-search/job-readiness component, length of time on AFDC, and JOBS program completion had a positive impact on earnings.

Our regression model had an F value of 60.419 and was significant at Alpha = .0001; however, this model provided little explanatory power with an R-square of only .1693. Our model results uncovered few relationships that were surprising. From our review of the existing body of research, we expected to find that greater work experience, higher educational levels, older participants' maturity, JOBS program completion, and participation in a job-search activity had a positive influence on earnings. We were slightly surprised that longer lengths of time spent on AFDC had a positive association with increased earnings; however, the significance of this relationship was questionable since it was not discernible at Alpha = .05.

In addition, we expected to find the participant's age at the time of the first child's birth, the number of children in the AFDC case, participation in a JOBS high school component, participation in post-secondary education, and JOBS participation in Kansas City all would have a negative impact on earnings. The negative relationship between educational activities and earnings might seem a little surprising. As discussed earlier in this chapter, however, when JOBS participants enroll in school activi-

TABLE 6-8

ORDINARY LEAST SQUARES REGRESSION STATISTICS—JOBS PARTICIPANTS

DEPENDENT VARIABLE = TOTAL EARNINGS   N = 5,935

INDEPENDENT VARIABLE	PARAM. EST.	STAND. EST.	STAND. ERROR	T	PROB> T
	-1,033.99	0.00	999.76	-1.03	0.3011
Area Specific Indicators					
County AFDC %	-35.64	-0.04	86.72	-0.41	0.6811
County unemployment rate	-47.47	-0.01	103.46	-0.46	0.6464
County poverty %	-3.26	-0.00	45.72	-0.07	0.9431
Number of JOBS case managers	19.53	0.07	17.41	1.12	0.2619
* St. Louis	872.35	0.11	355.89	2.45	0.0143
* Kansas City	-812.40	-0.08	337.93	-2.40	0.0162
Northeast Missouri	493.68	0.01	452.13	1.09	0.2749
Southeast Missouri	-423.40	-0.05	439.86	-0.96	0.3358
JOBS Participant Characteristics					
* Age	64.76	0.11	11.50	5.63	0.0001
Sex	310.54	0.01	336.45	0.92	0.3561
Race	164.78	0.02	138.80	1.19	0.2352
* Age at first child	-82.33	-0.09	18.42	-4.47	0.0001
* Educational level	306.22	0.12	35.58	8.61	0.0001
* Number of children	-266.23	-0.08	47.47	-5.61	0.0001
* Months work exp.	365.53	0.34	14.20	25.75	0.0001
** Length of stay on AFDC	2.66	0.02	1.53	1.74	0.0828
JOBS Component Activity					
* High school or GED	-326.93	-0.04	123.72	-2.64	0.0083
Skill/vocational training	-62.98	-0.00	172.49	-0.37	0.7150
** Post-secondary education	-390.23	-0.02	208.79	-1.87	0.0617
* Job readiness/job search	979.30	0.03	455.25	2.15	0.0315
** Participant completed JOBS	294.96	0.02	161.44	1.83	0.0678

TABLE 6-8 *CONTINUED*

F VALUE = 60.419   PROB > F = 0.0001

R-SQUARE = 0.1693   ADJUSTED R-SQUARE = 0.1665

NOTE: * Indicates significance at Alpha=.05
        ** Indicates significance at Alpha=.10
        Data are rounded.
DATA SOURCE: Missouri Department of Social Services, Research and Evaluation,
JOBS Research Data Set.

ties, they tend to drop out of the labor force, thus reducing their immediate earnings for greater future earnings—we hope—as a result of their increased education. Since the Kansas City JOBS program design also places an emphasis on educational activities and not on immediate job-search assistance, we would expect to see this phenomenon occurring in the Kansas City area.

Our major surprise was the low explanatory power of the model. While many of the independent variables included in the model were significant and contributed to an explanation of earnings/dependency, it is obvious that variables not included in the model provide more of an explanation. Possibly, factors such as self-esteem, individual motivation, appearance, promptness, family support, a particular job skill or skill level, health, racial prejudice, or intelligence have more of an impact on earnings than the variables we tested.

For instance, self-esteem is probably a major factor in labor market success. One of the criticisms we continually hear about welfare recipients concerns their lack of self-esteem. Often, welfare recipients have experienced many failures in life in order to get to the point where they are dependent on public charity. These recipients lack the confidence to keep trying and to handle rejection by potential employers. They may not have faith in their abilities, so continued job-search efforts may seem futile. Possibly, a measure of individual self-esteem in our model would have increased its explanatory power.

Similarly, individual motivation is another factor which probably contributes significantly to labor market success. When a single mother wants to demonstrate to her children that she is a capable person who can take care of them, she is likely to overcome previously insurmountable barriers. Conversely, the welfare recipient who desires to conform to the cultural "norm" of a welfare milieu is probably not going to strive for a change in circumstances. If we would have included a variable that measured the degree of individual motivation, we might also have had a more complete model.

The same is true for traits like appearance and promptness. Obviously, a clean, neat-looking individual who arrives on time will fare better in the work place than a sloppy, unwashed latecomer. Even health and intelligence may be important measures to include in a model. The single mother with chronic physical ailments or emotional problems will certainly be less prepared to enter the work force than an active, energetic woman, particularly if she also has small children. At the same time, an intelligent employee who uses good sense is more marketable by far than a person who lacks mental aptitude. All of these factors involve commonplace value judgments, and all are involved in employers' real-life decisions about hiring and retention. All of these factors, however, are also difficult to measure and to include in a model. Also, it goes without saying, that leaving potentially relevant variables out of the regression equation will theoretically result in biased estimates.

PARTICIPANTS WHO SUCCESSFULLY COMPLETE JOBS

To examine our fifth research question—Are the people who successfully complete JOBS and enter employment different from the individuals who participate in JOBS and do not enter employment?—we examined the key characteristics of four groups of JOBS participants: those who completed JOBS, those who completed JOBS and are employed, participants who completed JOBS and are not employed, and participants who dropped out of JOBS.

As table 6-9 indicates, of the 5,935 individuals who participated in JOBS during the first two years, 1,474 (or 24.8 percent) exited the program. Of the individuals who left JOBS, 632 (or 42.9 percent) completed their individual employability plan (IEP) while 842 individuals (57.1 percent) dropped out. Of the 632 individuals who completed JOBS, 26 (or 41.6 percent) left JOBS employed while 369 (or 58.4 percent) were not employed at the time they exited JOBS. The overall JOBS dropout rate during its first two years was 14.19 percent. JOBS staff felt this number was low and an indication of program satisfaction among participants, since 75.2 percent were still participating and 10 percent had already completed the program.

Compared to the total JOBS population, the group of individuals who exited JOBS after completing their individual employability plans contained fewer minority subjects, more males, were slightly older, had

TABLE 6-9

KEY JOBS PARTICIPANT CHARACTERISTICS—ALL REGIONS

VARIABLE	TOTAL JOBS	JOBS DROPOUT	EXITED COMPLETE	COMP. EMP.	COMP. JOBS NOT EMP.
N	5,935	842	632	263	369
RACE %					
WHITE	32.9	38.0	34.7	39.2	31.4
MINORITY	67.1	62.0	65.3	60.8	68.6
SEX %					
FEMALE	97.5	97.2	96.7	95.8	97.3
MALE	2.5	2.8	3.3	4.2	2.7
AVERAGE AGE	24.7	23.9	24.7	25.8	23.9
AVERAGE EDUCATION	11.2	11.1	11.4	11.7	11.2
AV. MONTHS WORK EXP.	2.5	2.5	2.8	3.4	2.4
AV. NUMBER OF CHILDREN	2.2	2.1	2.0	2.0	2.1
AVERAGE AGE BIRTH OF FIRST CHILD	19.7	19.5	20.0	20.5	19.7
AV. MONTHS ON AFDC	32.8	29.0	33.1	32.0	34.0

NOTE: Data may contain missing observations. Data are rounded. A total of 1,474 JOBS participants, or 24.8 percent, exited the program between July 1, 1990, and June 30, 1992.
SOURCE: Missouri Department of Social Services, Research and Evaluation, JOBS Research Data Set.

slightly more education, more work experience, slightly fewer children, and had waited longer to have their first child; however, they had received AFDC slightly longer. For JOBS subjects who exited the program, the differences in race, age, educational level, and parents age at first birth were discernible at Alpha = .05 as determined by either a Chi-square or F test of significance.

The characteristics of individuals who completed JOBS and were employed when they left the program exhibited a similar pattern to the group who completed their JOBS plan. The employed group generally contained fewer minorities, more males, individuals who are slightly older, more educated, have more work experience, fewer children, delayed child bearing longer, and have been on AFDC slightly less than JOBS subjects who completed their employability plan and were not employed when they exited JOBS. The race, age, education level, work experience, and age at birth of first child relationships were statistically significant at the .05 level.

Table 6-10 indicates overall JOBS completion rates compared to the percent of those completing JOBS who are employed at the time of

TABLE 6-10

JOBS Completion and Employment Rates—All Regions

Region	Total JOBS Subj.	Total Exited JOBS	Total JOBS Comp.	% Comp. Plan	Subjects Employed at Completion	% Comp. Plan Empl.
Total	5,935	1,474	632	42.9	263	41.6
Kansas City	959	225	88	39.1	30	34.1
Northeast	82	24	6	25.0	5	83.3
Southeast	1,803	518	223	43.1	91	35.3
St. Louis	3,091	707	315	44.6	137	49.8

Note: 75.2 percent of all JOBS participants were still participating in JOBS on June 30, 1992. Data may contain missing observations. Data are rounded.
Source: Missouri Department of Social Services, Research and Evaluation, JOBS Research Data Set.

completion, by region. As this table indicates, 75.2 percent of all JOBS participants were still in the program as of June 30, 1992. Of the individuals who left JOBS, 42.9 percent successfully completed their individual employability plan and 41.6 percent of the individuals who completed their IEP were employed when they left the program.

IS JOBS COST-EFFECTIVE?

To explore the sixth research question—Is the Missouri JOBS program cost-effective in its early years?—we will utilize a cost-benefit methodology focusing on wages earned and avoidance of AFDC benefit costs. Theoretically, if the JOBS program is succeeding at reducing dependency and encouraging self-sufficiency during the first two years, we would expect to see JOBS participants' labor market earnings increase and AFDC utilization decrease to a degree that offsets JOBS program expenditures. If JOBS is cost-effective during its first two years, we would expect to see the earnings of the individuals who participate in JOBS exceed those of the comparison group who did not participate. Likewise, we would expect the AFDC grants of JOBS participants to be lower than those of the non-JOBS subjects. We would also expect eventually to see more JOBS subjects than non-JOBS subjects exiting welfare. For JOBS to be cost-neutral or cost-effective during its first two years, we would expect to see the above relationships exist to a degree where the program costs are offset by JOBS participants' increased earnings and reduced AFDC grants, or exit from welfare.

Literature indicates, however, that at least in the early phases of employment and training programs, expenditures are not often offset by earnings and reductions in AFDC payments. In fact, the Manpower Demonstration Research Corporation (MDRC) evaluation studies of welfare employment and training programs from the 1980s indicate that these programs often cost more initially than they return in savings.[7]

The Manpower Demonstration Research Corporation (MDRC) findings also indicate the service delivery strategies utilized will have a bearing on early cost-benefit ratios. For instance, programs that rely heavily on job search and job placement have a higher potential to remove people from the welfare rolls immediately. Conversely, education and training components will encourage individuals to stay on AFDC until they complete their school or training—which can often take a year or more. The trade off in service delivery strategies is immediate, short-term gain versus the potential for a higher, long-term gain after a more costly investment in education and training.[8]

With regard to services offered, MDRC found that earnings impacts from both low-cost job search and higher cost programs were realized. A range of welfare-to-work programs—those that emphasize immediate job placement as well as those that provide some more intensive services—can produce sustained increases in employment and earnings for single parents on welfare. Employment and earnings results did not occur, however, when resources per eligible individual were too low to provide employment-directed assistance or when programs were operated in a rural, very weak labor market. Note, however, that measured in terms of impact per dollar invested, low-cost job-search/work-experience programs produced larger earnings gains and, to some extent, greater welfare savings than programs that emphasize higher-cost components, suggesting the existence of diminishing returns.[9]

While the MDRC findings are encouraging since they support the contention that training programs can increase the earnings of participants and lead to welfare savings, MDRC also concluded that "welfare-to-work programs usually benefited AFDC clients but *generally led to only modest increases in their measured income.*"[10] For example, in a recent evaluation of the California JOBS program, Greater Avenues to Independence (GAIN), MDRC found "surprisingly positive" results among a broad base of JOBS clients in six California counties.

In a report released April 23, 1992, MDRC found that the annual earnings for single parents who spent a year in the GAIN program were $271 higher than for members of a control group who were denied services. In addition, welfare payments for those in GAIN were reduced by $281 a year when compared to those in the control group. This means that the average GAIN participant earned an additional $22.58 a month and received $23.42 less a month in welfare. While these findings may be "surprisingly positive," they certainly are modest. There is no national evidence that welfare-to-work programs such as JOBS move a significant number of participants out of poverty or that the initial positive effects are sustained over the long term.[11]

In looking at the question of whether Missouri's JOBS program in particular is cost-effective, the Missouri JOBS program spent $12,130,547 to provide employment and training and support service to 8,815 JOBS participants during its first two years. These services were provided at an average cost of $1,376 per participant excluding day care costs.[12] (See appendix B.)

As table 6-1 indicates, JOBS participants earned an average of $2,253 during the above same two-year period while non-JOBS subjects earned an average of $4,685 or $2,432 more than the JOBS subjects. This means that people who participated in JOBS earned $1,216 less per year or $101.33 less per month than AFDC recipients who did not participate in JOBS. While the average earnings increased for individuals who completed JOBS training to $2,798, the non-JOBS group still earned an average of $1,887 more over the entire eight-quarter period or $78.63 more per month.

Part of the earnings difference between the JOBS and non-JOBS subjects may be related to the JOBS group being more destitute to begin with. Our research findings in chapter 5 reveal that, when compared to the non-JOBS group, JOBS participants possess characteristics that are more associated with dependency such as less work experience, longer lengths of time on AFDC, and more children in the family. In addition, as table 6-12 indicates, the JOBS subjects may also initially have less income than the non-JOBS comparison group.

When we compare the pre-JOBS quarterly earnings of JOBS and non-JOBS subjects in Kansas City during the year preceding the availability of JOBS—the third quarter of 1990 through the second quarter of 1991—we find that the non-JOBS subjects had significantly more earnings. For instance, in the third quarter of 1990, non-JOBS subjects earned an average of $694.94 compared to $412.58 for the JOBS group. This earnings pattern is consistent during all four pre-JOBS quarters and is statistically significant at Alpha = .05, according to ANOVA.

With regard to the JOBS subjects who completed their training, the non-JOBS subjects earned higher wages in every quarter except one. In the second quarter of 1992, individuals who completed JOBS earned an average of $668 while individuals in the non-JOBS group earned $592, a difference of $76. In addition, during this same quarter, individuals who completed JOBS and who were employed at the time of completion earned $1,269—$677 more than the non-JOBS subjects. It appears that JOBS participation, at least for the people who complete the program, is having a positive impact on earnings. (See tables 6-1 through 6-4 for area detail.)

Likewise, analysis of the available AFDC grant data indicates a similar pattern to the wage data. The JOBS subjects received an average AFDC grant of $246.85 compared to the grant for non-JOBS subjects of $227.22—or $19.63 higher. Again, we suspect that the JOBS subjects had higher AFDC grants because they were more destitute to begin with than the non-JOBS subjects. An analysis of the key individual characteristics and the pre-JOBS earnings data for the Kansas City area, cited earlier, supports this contention. The AFDC grants received by individuals who completed JOBS successfully, however, were somewhat lower. People completing JOBS successfully received an average AFDC grant of $211.85 compared to $227.22 for non-JOBS AFDC recipients—$15.37 lower. (See tables 6-5 and 6-7 for area detail.)

KANSAS CITY VERSUS ST. LOUIS

In our chapter 1 discussion of research question 7—Is there a significant difference in JOBS program outcomes for different geographic areas of Missouri?—we indicated the Missouri JOBS program allows for considerable local flexibility in both program design and implementation. As an example, the St. Louis City program was designed and implemented by staff from the Division of Family Services with minimal "outside" input. On the other hand, the Kansas City JOBS project was designed and implemented by an advisory committee of local citizens. The Kansas City Advisory Committee was appointed by Gary Stangler, director of the Department of Social Services, and it continues to function in an advisory and oversight role.

Data for the two sites are not totally comparable since St. Louis has been in operation for two years and Kansas City has only been operating one year. Moreover, population demographics and local economic conditions exhibit considerable variance. (See tables 4-1 through 4-4.) But the data do provide for some interesting comparisons.

With regard to the characteristics of the individuals served (see chapter 5), 78.3 percent of the St. Louis participants and 64.9 percent of the Kansas City participants belonged to one of the federal target groups. On average, St. Louis JOBS subjects are younger, less educated, have less work experience, and had their first child at an earlier age. They have received AFDC longer, have slightly fewer children in the family, and have more minority and women participants. These trends are representative of the difference in the overall AFDC population of the two areas, with St. Louis being noticeably more disadvantaged. (See table 6-11.)

With regard to outcomes of JOBS participants in the two areas, 88 of the 225 individuals, or 39.1 percent, who left JOBS in Kansas City completed the program, and 30 of these individuals were employed at the time of completion. In contrast, 707 exited JOBS in St. Louis with 315, or 44.6 percent, completing and 137 individuals employed at the time of completion. The 88 people who completed JOBS in Kansas City had total eighth-quarter average earnings of $3,262 versus $2,789 for the 315 St. Louis participants. As table 6-12 indicates, the eighth-quarter average earnings for the two areas suggest some interesting trends, especially for the participants who completed JOBS.

For instance, the St. Louis JOBS-completed group had average third quarter 1990 earnings—the first quarter the JOBS program was avail-

TABLE 6-11

CHARACTERISTICS OF JOBS AND NON-JOBS SUBJECTS

| | ST. LOUIS | | KANSAS CITY | |
	JOBS	NON-JOBS	JOBS	NON-JOBS
N	3,091	2,579	959	2,124
Federal Target Group	78.3%	53.9%	64.9%	38.7%
Age (years)	23.9	27.4	24.8	28.2
Education (years)	11.3	11.1	11.4	11.4
Mo. Work Exp. (last 12 mo.)	2.4	2.5	2.8	3.6
Age at First Birth	19.4	21.1	19.9	21.5
Time on AFDC (months)	35.4	36.7	25.9	22.5
Number of Children	2.2	2.2	2.3	2.0
Minority	90.1%	84.4%	72.6%	70.0%
Women	98.6%	96.4%	97.7%	93.2%

NOTE: Data are rounded.
SOURCE: Author's data, tables 5-1 through 5-11.

able—of $462.90. Their average quarterly earnings decreased gradually to $240.91 during the fourth quarter of the JOBS program—second quarter of 1991—probably reflecting a voluntary reduction in work effort and the individual's commitment to JOBS participation. Beginning with the third quarter of 1991, however, their average quarterly earnings started increasing until they reached a high point of $686.80 in the second quarter of 1992, the last quarter for which data are available.

The data for the Kansas City JOBS-completed subjects are even more interesting because four quarters of pre-JOBS data are also available. For this group of subjects, JOBS appears to have initially caused a

TABLE 6-12

AVERAGE EIGHT-QUARTER EARNINGS OF NON-JOBS SUBJECTS,
ALL JOBS PARTICIPANTS, AND PARTICIPANTS WHO COMPLETED JOBS
(ST. LOUIS AND KANSAS CITY)

QUARTER		NON-JOBS SUBJECTS		JOBS SUBJECTS (TOTAL)		JOBS SUBJECTS (COMPLETED)	
		STL ($)	KC ($)	STL ($)	KC ($)	STL ($)	KC ($)
	N	2,579	2,124	3,091	959	315	88
3-1990		567.63	694.94	328.96	412.58	462.90	503.20
4-1990		574.31	751.99	285.41	405.80	388.08	384.52
1-1991		527.08	674.16	235.11	257.73	255.56	307.11
2-2991		548.18	713.20	265.96	240.50	240.91	260.53
3-1991		555.88	684.97	286.41	183.20	290.99	129.19
4-1991		555.27	726.78	309.76	197.12	303.40	270.40
1-1992		522.74	681.37	307.35	178.26	339.97	508.34
2-1992		560.66	701.58	405.21	262.96	686.80	898.70

NOTE: Data may contain missing observations. Data are rounded.
SOURCE: Missouri Department of Social Services, Research and Evaluation, JOBS Research Data Set.

considerable reduction in work wages. The Kansas City JOBS-completed subjects averaged quarterly earnings of $503.20 during the third quarter 1990, one year before JOBS was available in the Kansas City area. During the third quarter 1991, the starting point for JOBS in Kansas City, however, average earnings for this group dropped to $129.19.

On a positive note, within four quarters the average quarterly earnings of this group increased to $898.70. During the first year of the JOBS program in the Kansas City area, average quarterly earnings of the JOBS-completed group increased from $129.19 to $898.70. Similarly, over the two-year period, the St. Louis JOBS participants increased their average quarterly earnings from $462.90 to $686.80.

When we compare the quarterly earnings of the JOBS population in both St. Louis and Kansas City after one year of program operation, we find the earnings of the aggregate St. Louis subjects decreased from $328.96 in the first quarter of JOBS to $265.96 in the fourth quarter. In contrast, the Kansas City subjects exhibited an increase from $183.20 during the first quarter to $262.96 during the fourth quarter of program operation. For the individuals who completed JOBS, the differences were even more dramatic. The earnings of St. Louis participants who completed JOBS decreased from $462.90 during the first quarter to $260.91 in the fourth quarter of JOBS, while Kansas City participants increased from $129.19 to $898.70 over a four-quarter period.

Indications are JOBS participation has improved the earnings of the aggregate group of JOBS subjects who complete the program. It is also apparent that the earnings gains are more dramatic in the Kansas City area.

Theoretically, the early involvement of community leaders in the local JOBS planning and implementation process along with its continued participation in an advisory role may have provided the Kansas City program an early qualitative edge. In addition to benefiting from the experience and insights of the advisory committee members, the Kansas City JOBS program also gained access to some of Kansas City's better employers. Moreover, the advisory committee was able to form early collaborative linkages with several well-respected private and not-for-profit social service agencies.

The oversight and evaluation role assumed by the advisory committee also appears to have generated greater interest in more diverse program outcome measures than the population participation and target group participation percentages required by the Department of Health and Human Services. Local JOBS management staff are periodically required to provide the advisory committee with data about caseload levels, number of JOBS graduates entering employment, employment wage rates, and job retention rates. This aspect of committee involvement appears to have "focused" the Kansas City JOBS staff on employment-related outcomes and positive program benefits. The committee's continuing oversight role may serve to reinforce this focus.

Considering the differences in the length of time the program has been in operation in the two areas, the differences in the characteristics of the population being served, and particularly the differences in local economic conditions, we feel conclusions about the effectiveness or desirability of one delivery system over another are inappropriate. This topic deserves additional study.

THE POTENTIAL OF VOCATIONAL EDUCATION

As mentioned earlier, it can be argued that the traditional approach for evaluating dependency is geared toward the status quo, or short term. A more realistic view that truly reflects the idea of helping people over the long term, should incorporate the future value of education and possibly even the satisfaction of the participants. For instance, an individual's satisfaction with her or his activity might also be a nontraditional indicator of program success. In a recent survey of one hundred JOBS individuals selected randomly from St. Louis and southeast Missouri, the Reform Organization for Welfare (ROWEL) found that 55 percent of all JOBS participants were very satisfied and 36 percent were somewhat satisfied with the FUTURES program. Seven percent were somewhat dissatisfied and 2 percent were very dissatisfied with FUTURES.

In addition, 85 percent of the participants felt the program was having either a positive or very positive effect on their children while 6 percent felt the program's effect was either negative or very negative. Nine percent indicated FUTURES participation had no effect on their children.[13]

In one "MacNeil/Lehrer News Hour," correspondent Paul Solman focused on the retraining of workers in technical occupations with demand such as the air conditioning, health care, or culinary trades. Solman and his guests pointed out that laid-off workers and older workers can learn new and different job skills that provide the potential for well-paid jobs.[14] Vocational training through the Missouri JOBS program has provided similar results. For example, a sample of 773 recent JOBS and JTPA classroom training graduates from the vocational programs operated by the three campuses of the St. Louis junior college district and the University of Missouri-St. Louis found that the graduates earned average hourly starting wages of $13.23, $16.39, $14.92, and $15.64 respectively. (See table 6-13.) Many of these graduates participated in health care and medical technology training.

TABLE 6-13

AVERAGE HOURLY STARTING WAGES OF JOBS/JPTA PARTICIPANTS BY SELECTED TRAINING INSTITUTIONS

LOCATION	ENROLLEES	TERMINATIONS	ENTERED EMPLOYEMENT	AVERAGE WAGE
M.U.-St. Louis	100	30	26	$15.64
Forest Park C.C.	365	164	84	$13.23
Meramec C.C.	115	58	34	$16.39
Flo. Valley C.C.	193	65	50	$14.92
Penn.Valley C.C.	444	300	219	$ 6.59
Mineral Area C.C.	107	78	46	$ 5.08
Three Rivers C.C.	81	36	14	$ 4.58
Columbia AVTS	69	51	39	$ 7.49
Poplar Bluff AVTS	45	26	18	$ 6.08
Cape Girar. AVTS	145	122	87	$ 5.23
Kennett AVTS	41	27	13	$ 4.99
Pike/Lincoln AVTS	68	40	28	$ 5.69
	N = 1,773	N = 997	N = 658	

NOTE: AVTS = Area Vocational Technical School; C.C. = Community College
SOURCE: Department of Elementary and Secondary Education Internal Report, FY 92 Skill Training Performance, May 1993.

In contrast, classroom training program graduates from rural area vocational technical schools (ATVS) receive average beginning wages in the $5–$7.50 range while high school graduates without some college or vocational training receive average beginning wages in the minimum-wage range of $4.25–$5 per hour.[15] Again, graduates of health care programs such as nursing and medical technology tend to receive higher hourly starting wages of $8–$12 depending on area and demand.[16]

According to Dr. Rush Robinson, of the St. Louis College of Health Carriers, the medical industry is in such need of trained employees that most of their students receive several job offers and are placed prior to graduation. The medical industry is very competitive, and most jobs offer a good benefit package which often contains provisions for employees to continue to upgrade their education at the employer's expense. In fact, university-affiliated hospitals in the St. Louis area pay the employee's school tuition and the tuition of their children through graduate school.[17] JOBS graduates from these programs have both the skills and earnings potential to eventually become self-sufficient.

The Missouri JOBS program places an emphasis on human capital investment and emphasizes educational activities such as completing high school or its equivalent, along with post-secondary school and skill training. These educational activities last at least one year and frequently longer. As of June 30, 1992, over 70 percent of all JOBS participants were enrolled in educational activities.[18] JOBS field staff believe that many of the people who enroll in educational components make a commitment to completing their education and voluntarily reduce their labor force participation.

There is also considerable evidence that the investment in education will pay off in the long run. In a 1987 report issued by the Department of Elementary and Secondary Education (DESE), *The Longitudinal Follow-up of 1981 Missouri High School Graduates,* DESE followed a sample of high school graduates for five years and compared the experiences of vocational-technical students with those of their traditional high school counterparts. The study found vocational graduates earn more money than non-vocational graduates. Data show that vocational graduates exhibit a 15–20 percent annual salary advantage over non-vocational graduates. The study also found that the vocational graduates had greater job stability, higher employment rates, and held full-time jobs at a higher rate—92 percent versus 74 percent for the non-vocational graduates. The study also found that the majority of vocational graduates worked in an area related to their training, and were more confident of their ability to compete for jobs than the non-vocational graduates; 80 percent of vocational graduates indicated they were satisfied with their current or most recent job.[19]

In a recent study, *Pathways to Employment*, the Washington State Institute for Public Policy found that women on welfare who enroll in vocational education and training programs increase their chances of getting a job and leaving the welfare rolls by 78 percent. The report found that vocational education and training, when analyzed in combination with all other variables, had a statistically significant effect on landing a job. The authors of the report summarized the positive results arising from vocational education and training, noting "the report's findings have interesting implications for welfare-to-work programs. States should place a particular emphasis on vocational education and training when designing their Job Opportunities and Basic Skills Training Programs (JOBS)."[20]

THE WELFARE POPULATION

During this study we had the opportunity to talk to many Division of Family Services employees, both JOBS staff and Income Maintenance staff. When asked to evaluate JOBS, staff members were generally enthusiastic about their program and talked freely about their successes and failures. JOBS staff possess few illusions about the difficulty of their mission and the people they work with. They generally perceive AFDC recipients as being close to the bottom rung of the economic ladder—one step above the homeless. To receive AFDC a person has to prove she or he is poor. Most are not working, or they work sporadic low-wage jobs often without the benefits of paid leave and health insurance. AFDC recipients own few assets; legally they cannot have available resources above $1,000, and their car, if they own one, cannot be worth more than $1,500. Often they live in substandard housing and have problems paying their heat and electric bills. Many lack a basic high school education, and many others have health problems or have a child with health problems that requires them to stay on AFDC in order to receive their Medicaid card. Their total package of benefits—AFDC, food stamps, etc.—still leaves them below the poverty line. The one thing they all have in common is that they all have children, children who are growing up in poverty.

In addition to being poor, many of the people receiving AFDC have other problems which compound their poverty and their dependency on the welfare system. Many grew up in poor or dysfunctional families and have dysfunctional families of their own. Many of the women tell stories of abusive home environments when they were children. Many have lived with or are living with an abusive partner. Many made bad decisions early in life such as dropping out of school, or having a child too early, or becoming dependent on drugs or alcohol. Some have mental problems; others are border-line functional. Many of their lives are so tenuous that a minor crises such as a sick child, or a disagreement with a co-worker or supervisor, will cause them to quit a job or training activity. Many have not learned to deal with the circumstances that most middle-class working people consider normal, everyday occurrences.

Because of the multitude of problems AFDC recipients face, individual successes on occasion are temporary. JOBS participants make a few strides forward only to take an occasional stride backward. While there are indications that JOBS participation can increase earnings, and we have numerous stories about JOBS participants obtaining good jobs and leaving welfare, we remain only cautiously optimistic. JOBS offers the potential to turn some lives around and the chance for some to move from poverty to a better life, but many of the participants need more help than just an education and marketable job skills.

FINDINGS

With regard to our third research question—Does JOBS participation result in increased labor force participation and decreased public assistance utilization?—we find little evidence to support the contention that JOBS participation has resulted in increased labor force participation, at least for the entire JOBS population in the first two years of the program. Therefore, we reject hypothesis 4: There is no statistically significant difference between the labor force participation of JOBS subjects and that of non-JOBS subjects. As stated earlier, however, we feel our methodology and the limited two-year time period for which we have data is biased toward this finding. We would have been surprised to find anything else.

We reject hypothesis 5: There is no statistically significant difference between the AFDC grant amount received by JOBS subjects and that received by non-JOBS subjects. Tables 6-5 and 6-6 show there are significant differences between the AFDC grants of the non-JOBS population, JOBS subjects, and JOBS subjects who have completed the program. While the most recent AFDC grants of the aggregate JOBS population are $19.63 higher than the sample of non-JOBS subjects, the grants of JOBS participants who complete the program average $15.37 less. During our examination of research question 4 to identify which JOBS activities have the most impact on reduced AFDC dependency, we found that participation in job-search/job-readiness activities had the most significant positive immediate impact on short-term increased earnings. Therefore, we reject hypothesis 6 that participation in a specific JOBS activity component does not result in increased labor force participation or reduced AFDC utilization, at least in the short term.

An examination of research question 5—Are the people who successfully complete JOBS and enter employment different from the individuals who participate in JOBS and do not enter employment?—leads one to reject hypothesis 7 that there is no significant difference between the characteristics of individuals who complete JOBS training and seek employment and those who do not. Individuals who complete JOBS have certain characteristics, as explained earlier, which differentiate them from people who do not complete the program's components. They tend to be slightly older, better educated, have more work experience, have fewer children, and delayed having their first child longer than JOBS participants who dropped out of the program. In other words, people who complete JOBS tend to have fewer barriers to participation than people who drop out of the program. It appears the people who are dropping out may be the group most in need of JOBS since they tend to possess more of the attributes associated with welfare dependency.

When we originally contemplated devising a cost-benefit methodology to address research question 6, we planned to compare the experiences of the experimental group, JOBS participants, with those of the comparison group, non-JOBS participants, to determine each group's average wages and average AFDC grants. The purpose was to construct a rudimentary cost-benefit methodology based on cost avoidance: that is, if JOBS training is having a short-term significant positive impact, we would expect JOBS individuals to earn more wages and receive less AFDC than non-JOBS counterparts. The differences in AFDC grants and earnings could then be used to calculate program benefits in comparison to program costs.[21]

Evidence to date, however, does not support the contention that JOBS training has resulted in increased earnings and lower grants for a substantial portion of JOBS participants—at least during the first two years of JOBS. The aggregate gains in earnings and lower AFDC grants exhibited by individuals who complete JOBS appear to have been more than offset by the total JOBS training costs and aggregate increased AFDC grants and decreased earnings. We have not attempted to develop a cost-benefit methodology beyond demonstrating that JOBS gains in wages earned and lower AFDC costs have not materialized for most JOBS participants. Again, this is not surprising since the majority of all JOBS participants enrolled during the first two years—75.2 percent—are still in the program. They have not had time to complete the program, find employment, and demonstrate decreased welfare dependency. Consequently, we accept hypothesis 8: In its first two years, JOBS is not cost-effective.

In addressing research question 7—Is there a significant difference in JOBS program outcomes for different geographic areas of Missouri?—we find there are regional variances in JOBS participant characteristics and program outcomes as shown in tables 6-7, 6-11, and 6-12. These regional differences are particularly evident in our comparison of St. Louis and Kansas City. As the data on table 6-12 indicate, after one year of JOBS program operation, individuals who complete JOBS in Kansas City are earning $898.70 versus $240.91 for the St. Louis subjects. Therefore, we reject hypothesis 9 that there are no significant regional differences in program outcomes—labor force participation and AFDC grant amounts.

At the beginning of this chapter, we asked the question, Are the people who participate in JOBS less dependent on the public welfare system than people who do not participate in JOBS? Our answer is a definitive "probably"! During this study we have found that AFDC recipients who complete JOBS do exhibit an increase in earned wages and a decrease in AFDC benefits. We found this trend developed late in the data series, during the eighth and last quarter for which we had participant wage data; however, we found even more positive results when we examined individual local JOBS projects.

For instance, during our comparison of subjects who completed JOBS in St. Louis City and Kansas City, we found that the St. Louis subjects showed marked earnings gains during the eighth quarter of program availability in their area. Similarly, the Kansas City subjects showed noted improvement during the fourth quarter of program availability in their area. In fact, the earnings of the Kansas City JOBS subjects after four quarters of participation were over twice as high as the St. Louis subjects after eight quarters of participation.

Hypothetically, there are three initial apparent explanations that account for the difference in the extent of the wage gains. The first is that the Kansas City economy is considerably healthier than in St. Louis, thus providing greater employment opportunities for JOBS graduates. Data presented in chapter 4 supports this theory. Secondly, the Kansas City JOBS population is "less disadvantaged" than the St. Louis population; therefore, they have fewer labor force barriers and are more likely to find employment sooner. Data presented in chapter 5 supports this contention. And finally, the Kansas City program design, with continuing involvement and oversight by the Kansas City Advisory Committee, has resulted in a superior JOBS delivery strategy. We find it conceivable that a combination of all three factors account for the differences in the earnings gains between the two areas.

Despite the limitations of our data series discussed earlier, we believe our findings indicate there is a genuine potential for people who complete JOBS to increase their earnings and decrease their dependency on the public welfare system. Evaluations of other states' JOBS programs are also finding some positive results. This topic, however, warrants additional study.

NOTES

1. FUTURES is the name of Missouri's JOBS program.

2. Kevin Faust, Missouri Division of Family Services, Management Services Section, interview with author, 1993, to discuss "Internal Expenditure Tracking Report, Fiscal Years 1991 and 1992." Child-care expenditures are not limited to JOBS participants. Federal JOBS regulations allow states to spend JOBS child-care funds on non-JOBS individuals who are participating in education, training, and employment activities who are not enrolled in the JOBS program.

3. We recognize that quarterly wages may not be the "perfect" measure of reduced welfare dependency. Other indicators such as employment rates, hours worked, and post-JOBS employment data might provide a good indication of reduced welfare dependency. We used the quarterly wage data because they do have certain advantages. Theoretically, if study subjects are working, by law, with few exceptions, their wages will be reported by their employers to the Missouri Division of Employment Security. These wage data are contained on a computer file, and they are perceived to be accurate and consistent since they are used by a government agency to determine an employer's tax liability and to disburse unemployment insurance benefits. Theoretically, quarterly wage data provide an indication of work and earnings; plus, we are able to use considerably larger samples than if we were forced to send out a survey questionnaire. Use of Employment Security wage data, while not perfect, allows us to avoid some of the problems associated with traditional survey research. Also, by "less need" we do not imply that a single mother with children, who is working and earns just enough to make her ineligible for AFDC payments, has significantly less economic need than a person who receives AFDC. Many individuals in this situation are still poor and are often referred to as the "working poor." In this context, "less need" relates to state AFDC eligibility guidelines where the people with the least income are considered most in need of assistance.

4. Ideally, this type of evaluation study would be more appropriate when long-term data are available, that is, after five to ten years of program availability when the experiences of program participants and graduates could be analyzed. As stated earlier, however, we believe there is a need to initiate program evaluation earlier in order to start identifying early trends and potential problems. Also, we feel policymakers are hesitant to support multimillion dollar appropriations if program evaluation

is not occurring.

5. By less dependent we mean that a greater share of the individual's total income package is derived from wages as opposed to government transfer payments such as AFDC.

6. For a discussion of individual characteristics that contribute to poverty and dependency see Irwin Garfinkel, "Welfare Policy In America," Institute for Research on Poverty, University of Wisconsin-Madison, Discussion Paper No. 847-87 (October 1987), 1–3; Irwin Garfinkel and Sara S. McLanahan, *Single Mothers and Their Children: A New American Dilemma?* (Washington, D.C.: Urban Institute, 1986), chap. 2.; Greg Duncan and Saul Hoffman, "The Use and Effects of Welfare: A Survey of Recent Evidence," paper presented at the conference on The Political Economy of the Transfer Society, Tallahassee, Florida (November 1987), 3–7; Mary Jo Bane and David Ellwood, "The Dynamics of Dependence and the Routes to Self-Sufficiency," *Final Report to the Department of Health and Human Services* (Cambridge, MA: Harvard University, Kennedy School of Government, 1983); David T. Ellwood, "The Origins of 'Dependency': Choices, Confidence, or Culture?" *Focus* 12 (Spring/Summer 1989): 6–13; and David T. Ellwood, "Targeting the Would-be Long-term Recipient of AFDC: Who Should Be Served?" Preliminary Report, Harvard University, 1985.

7. David A. Long, "The Budgetary Implications of Welfare Reform: Lessons From Four State Initiatives," *Journal of Policy Analysis and Management* 7 (1988): 295–296.

8. Judith M. Gueron and Edward Pauly, *From Welfare to Work* (New York: Russell Sage Foundation, 1991), 26.

9. Ibid., 34.

10. Ibid., 33.

11. *Welfare to Work*, (Washington, D.C.: MII Publications, April 27, 1992), 1.

12. Missouri Department of Social Services, *Outcome Measures, 1991–1992 Report* (December 29, 1992), 25. Day-care costs were also excluded because the Division of Family Services does not have a "clean" breakout of JOBS participants and day-care costs. Any AFDC recipient who participates in an educational or employment and training activity similar to JOBS is entitled to day care for their children, provided funds are available.

13. Reform Organization for Welfare and The Coalition on Human Needs, *FUTURES Survey of 100 FUTURES Participants* (March

1992).

14. "MacNeil/Lehrer News Hour," WNET, Show No. 4599 (April 5, 1993).

15. Randall Clark, Labor Market Analyst, Missouri Department of Labor and Industrial Relations, Division of Employment Security, interview with author, 1 July 1993.

16. Donald Eisinger, Director of Employment and Training Programs, Missouri Department of Elementary and Secondary Education, interview with author, 1993, to discuss data from an internal JTPA management information report generated in April 1993.

17. Dr. Rush Robinson, St. Louis College of Health Carriers, interview with author, 5 February 1993.

18. Missouri Division of Family Services, *FUTURES Monthly Management Information Report* (June 30, 1992).

19. The Missouri Department of Elementary and Secondary Education, *The Longitudinal Follow-up of 1981 High School Graduates* (Jefferson City, Missouri, October 1987).

20. State of Washington Institute for Public Policy, *Pathways to Employment* (Olympia, Washington, May 1993).

21. We realize that we are taking a very narrow approach in calculating program benefits based solely on quarterly earnings and reduced average welfare grant amounts. For instance, the benefits derived from increased education may not materialize immediately but at some time in the future. Also, benefits other than reduced welfare dependency may occur such as future reduced poverty, reduced criminal activity, or reduced use of alternative systems. See Peter Kemper, David A. Long, and Craig Thornton, *Supported Work Evaluation: Final Benefit-Cost Analysis* (New York: Manpower Demonstration Research Corporation, 1981).

VII

Recent Developments, 1993–1996:
Meaningful Reform or Political Symbolism?

> Block grants represent a substantial departure in social
> policy, moving us from the concept of a safety net to
> which all in need are entitled to the concept of life-
> boats, with only so much room (money).[1]

Most people in this country believe that the existing Aid to Families with Dependent Children (AFDC) program needs reforming with the
same certainty that they believe taxes are too high. Current welfare reform proposals cover the full spectrum from eliminating the AFDC system entirely so people will go to work, to increasing AFDC benefits so
families will have a higher standard of living. A few dissenters advocate
the cheapest solution to the welfare problem is to do nothing, believing
that writing a check is far less costly than actually reforming the system,
while diehard iconoclasts question whether meaningful reform is even
possible or desirable in the current political environment.

This chapter examines recent federal legislation that has been enacted to replace the JOBS program and "end welfare as we know it." It
also looks at state welfare reform initiatives, known as 1115 Waivers, in
which the Department of Health and Human Services (HHS) gives states
permission to deviate from federal laws and regulations.

155

THE PERSONAL RESPONSIBILITY AND WORK OPPORTUNITY ACT OF 1996

During the 1992 presidential election, candidate Bill Clinton promised to "end welfare as we know it." Four years later, welfare reform continues to be a major national election issue. For instance, national Republican campaign commercials have criticized President Clinton for giving welfare benefits to illegal immigrants while Democrat campaign ads have implied that President Clinton has accomplished the amazing feat of welfare reform.

At the state level, welfare issues such as immigrants receiving public assistance in California, or "grant capping" in New Jersey, have continued to flood the airwaves. State campaign ads have featured one party taking credit for reducing welfare rolls, or making people work for welfare, or denying additional benefits for additional children, and so forth, while the opposing party has claimed its candidates have better ideas about reforming welfare and the opponents have not been tough enough.

As both political parties have vied to take credit for reforming welfare, two main reform approaches have materialized: H.R. 3734, The Personal Responsibility and Work Opportunity Act of 1996, and the 1115 Waiver process where the federal Department of Health and Human Services grants states permission to experiment on their own with changing the welfare system. The first approach has been driven by a Republican-controlled Congress and the second by a Democrat presidential administration.

THE TEMPORARY ASSISTANCE FOR NEEDY FAMILIES BLOCK GRANT

During the week of December 18,1995, both houses of Congress endorsed a welfare reform conference committee agreement based on H.R. 4, the Personal Responsibility and Work Opportunity Act of 1995 (PRWO-95). While President Clinton vetoed this proposal in January 1996, the second welfare reform veto of his presidency, Title I of the bill, The Temporary Assistance for Needy Families Block Grant (TANF), represented congressional consensus for reforming welfare and evolved into H.R. 3734, the Personal Responsibility and Work Opportunity Act of 1996 (PRWO-96). This bill, which includes TANF, passed both houses of Congress during the first week of August 1996, and was signed "reluctantly" by President Clinton on August 22, 1996.[2]

This new law represents a major change in U.S. social policy by ending the entitlement status of Aid to Families with Dependent Children and shifting decision making about supporting the poor from Washington to the states. TANF repeals Titles IV-A and IV-F of the Social Security Act, thereby ending the entitlement status of both the Aid to Families with Dependent Children (AFDC) program, and the Family Support Act of 1988 (FSA), Job Opportunities and Basic Skills Training Program, which were previous modifications to the Social Security Act. In their place, states will divide a block grant of approximately $16.38 billion per year for each federal fiscal year from 1997–2001. Each state's share of the $16.38 billion block grant is based on its historical expenditures for AFDC, JOBS, and Energy Assistance (EA) programs.

The TANF block grant can be used by states in "any manner reasonably calculated to accomplish the purpose of TANF." This includes providing home energy assistance to low-income families and any activities that were authorized by Titles IV-A (AFDC) and IV-F (JOBS) of the Social Security Act on September 30, 1995. Also, PRWO-96 allows states the flexibility to transfer 30 percent of the TANF grant to support adoption and child-care programs as long as the funds are used in accordance with existing federal regulations governing those programs. TANF also places a 15 percent cap on the amount of funds a state can use for administration of programs, though the cap excludes the information technology and computerization necessary to track and monitor recipients.

In addition, TANF establishes several funds states can use in the event of an economic emergency: a contingency fund of two billion dollars over five years for states experiencing an economic downturn; a "rainy day" fund of $1.7 billion in federal loans to assist families and fund welfare-fraud prevention activities; a one-billion-dollar fund to provide performance bonuses to "high performing states"; a fund of eight hundred million dollars to assist states with unexpectedly high population growth; and a grant program which would provide bonuses to states that reduce out-of-wedlock birth rates without increasing abortions.

To receive the TANF grant, states must agree to a maintenance-of-effort provision, requiring states to continue spending at least 75-80 percent of the historical state General Revenue expenditures previously required to match pre-TANF federal funds. This provision allows states to reduce the amount of state money spent on the poor.

The second major provision of TANF is the imposition of a five-year time limit for receiving AFDC. Families can receive TANF assistance from block grant funds for only five years, although 20 percent of the average monthly caseload could exceed the five-year time limit for reasons of hardships or if the family includes an individual who "has been battered or subjected to extreme cruelty." States also have the option to provide less than five years of assistance if they wish.

In addition, TANF attempts to correct some of the perceived flaws of current AFDC legislation by allowing states to have "family caps" that prohibit the expenditure of block grant funds to support a child who was born while the family was already receiving assistance. TANF would also prohibit spending block grant funds to support illegal immigrants, families without a minor child or a pregnant woman, unmarried teen parents who do not live at home or in an approved adult-supervised setting, fugitive felons, and individuals who have been convicted of a drug-related felony. Also, individuals who refuse to cooperate in establishing paternity must have their TANF grant reduced by 25 percent.

WORK REQUIREMENTS

TANF requires a significant number of the individuals to participate in "allowable work activities." Beginning in fiscal year 1997, 25 percent of all parents in families receiving assistance would be required to participate in an allowable work activity. By fiscal year 2002, 50 percent of these individuals must participate. During fiscal year 1997, 75 percent of all individuals from two-parent families would have to participate in a work activity, with 90 percent participating by fiscal year 1999.

TANF defines allowable work activities as unsubsidized employment, subsidized private sector employment, subsidized public sector employment, work experience if private sector employment is not available, on-the-job-training, community service employment, job-search and job-readiness assistance for up to six weeks, job-skills training directly related to employment, education directly related to employment for recipients who have not completed high school, and secondary school attendance for anyone under age twenty who has not finished high school. TANF would allow one year of vocational school to count toward the work requirement; however, no more than 20 percent of individuals participating in TANF may participate in vocational education. In addition, TANF prohibits providing assistance to anyone between the ages of twenty and fifty if the person does not have or is not working toward a secondary school diploma or its equivalent.

In order to count toward the state's participation rate in fiscal year 1997, individuals from two-parent families would have to participate a minimum of thirty-five hours a week in one of the above activities, and single parents would be required to participate twenty hours. By fiscal year 2000, single parents must also be participating thirty hours per week. If individuals refuse to participate in work activities for the required number of hours, TANF allows states to reduce or terminate assistance.

In comparison to the present JOBS program, TANF requires more AFDC recipients to participate for more hours in an activity, allows for fewer participation exemptions, and gives states more flexibility to punish people who do not participate. Moreover, TANF focuses on work activities where JOBS has tended to focus on educational activities and allowed a greater variety of non-work-related activities to count toward federal participation requirements.

OTHER PROVISIONS

The Personal Responsibility and Work Opportunity Act of 1996 (PRWO-96) also consolidates all child-care assistance funding into one block grant through amendments to the Child Care and Development Block Grant (CCDBG). Existing programs such as AFDC, At-Risk, JOBS, and Transitional Child Care as well as some smaller programs are consolidated into the CCDBG. Funding would be guaranteed—a total of $13.9 billion over a six-year period, with discretionary funding of one billion dollars annually for fiscal years 1997–2002.

States that fail to meet all TANF requirements, can be penalized by having their block grant amount reduced. For instance, any state that "intentionally violates" TANF provisions could have its grant reduced by 5 percent. There is also a 4 percent penalty for failing to report required administrative data; a 5 percent penalty for not meeting work participation rates and a 2 percent penalty each additional year rates are not achieved with a maximum total penalty of 21 percent; a 2 percent penalty for failure to participate in an income and eligibility verification system; an additional 1–5 percent for substantial failure to comply with child-support enforcement requirements; and a 5 percent grant reduction if states exceed the five-year limit on paying TANF benefits. Total penalties in one year, however, cannot exceed 25 percent.

While Title I of the Personal Responsibility and Work Opportunity Act of 1996 will have the most impact on programs, several other titles have the potential to significantly change the social welfare system in this country, such as Title II, Supplemental Security Income (SSI); Title III, Child Support; Title IV, Restricting Welfare and Public Benefits for Aliens; Title V, Child Protection Block Grant Program, and Foster Care and Adoption Assistance; Title VI, Child Care; Title VII, Child Nutrition Programs; Title VIII, Food Stamps and Commodity Distribution Program; and Title IX, Miscellaneous provisions.

It should be noted that President Clinton also proposed legislation to reform the welfare system. The Clinton administration's Work and Responsibility Act, proposed changes to the welfare system by requiring work from public assistance recipients but did not end the entitlement status of AFDC or consolidate funds in block grants to the states. The president's bill also imposed a five-year time limit but allows more exclusions than the Republican bill.

STATE WELFARE REFORM EXPERIMENTS— 1115 WAIVER PROCESS

While the Clinton administration submitted its own welfare reform legislative package in the form of the Work and Responsibility Act, it did not receive serious consideration. The administration's main effort to reform welfare prior to passage of PRWO-96 has been working with the states through the U.S. Department of Health and Human Services and the 1115 Waiver process. This waiver process allows states to experiment with changes to their state AFDC system after obtaining HHS approval. Basically, Titles IV-A and IV-F of the Social Security Act require all states to administer the AFDC and JOBS programs according to rules and regulations established by HHS. Through a 1115 Waiver, states are essentially asking permission from HHS to deviate from existing federal law. In administering the programs, states must match federal funds at a rate that varies according to the activities a state performs. Some activities are matched at a rate of 90 percent federal funds to 10 percent state funds while other activities are matched at a 50 percent-to-50 percent rate.

If states wish to implement innovations with their welfare system, they must submit a 1115 Waiver to HHS describing what they want to do, expected outcomes, and expected costs. If HHS approves a state waiver for an experiment, which can typically last from five to ten years, the state must prove the experiment will not be more costly to the Federal government than the existing system. In the event the state experiment costs more than what would normally have been expended, the state is required to reimburse the U.S. government from state funds. Also, states are required to contract with an outside, unbiased party to perform a "rigorous evaluation" of the waiver. Normally, HHS equates "rigorous evaluation" with the use of an experimental research design.

Approximately forty states are presently experimenting with their state welfare systems through 1115 Waivers. While the Clinton administration appears to be encouraging the process, the George Bush administration should be given credit for originally promoting waivers. According to Michael Wiseman, in the January 1992 "State of the Union Address," President Bush encouraged states to continue a movement to replace the assumptions of the welfare state and help reform the welfare system. "We are going to help this movement," Bush said. "Often, state reform requires waiving certain federal regulations. I will act to make that process easier and quicker for every state that asks for our help."[3] When President Bush left office, eleven states had received HHS approval for waivers.[4]

Considerable duplication exists in current state waivers. For instance, approximately thirty states are experimenting with increasing the amount of money an AFDC recipient may earn or assets a family may accumulate before losing AFDC eligibility. Under existing law, the family AFDC grant is reduced one dollar for every dollar the family earns after standard income disregards expire, normally four to twelve months after the family starts earning income.[5] Other benefits, such as health insurance through Medicaid and possibly child-care assistance are also tied to AFDC eligibility. So once the family loses AFDC eligibility it may lose Medicaid and child-care assistance, unless members are categorically eligible to receive AFDC for other reasons.

The end result is a phenomena known as the "cliff effect." As long as the family has no income, it receives AFDC, Medicaid, food stamps, and other government benefits such as child care, energy assistance, and possibly housing assistance. Once the family earns a certain amount, AFDC ends and often other assistance also abruptly ends—the "cliff effect." As discussed earlier, the economic benefits derived from working, combined with the loss of leisure time and direct supervision of children, often does not offset the loss of the public assistance benefit package. (See discussion in chapter 3, "The Economics of Public Assistance" and table 3-4.) If a family is able to work and earn more income while reducing its AFDC check gradually, and keep Medicaid, child-care assistance and other benefits tied to AFDC, the family can build work experience and possibly a cushion of assets, which can help it permanently leave welfare behind.

Approximately thirty states have implemented waivers that impose some type of time limit on receipt of AFDC; however, the type of limit on benefits varies considerably from state to state. For instance, after thirty months, Vermont imposes a mandatory work requirement on recipients as a condition of further assistance. Colorado can terminate AFDC benefits after two years if a parent refuses to participate in job training, a work activity, or other state-mandated activity. Beginning in 1997, Missouri will limit adult benefits to twenty-four months, which can be extended to forty-eight months if necessary. Individuals who have received AFDC for thirty-six months and who sign self-sufficiency pacts and leave AFDC, are not eligible for additional benefits.[6]

In many of the states, the time limits apply to the adults receiving benefits, but children can still receive assistance, often with a reduced grant amount. Some states also have mandatory work, job training, or transition assistance programs that AFDC recipients must participate in as a condition of continued assistance after specified time limits are reached. In other states, time limits on receiving assistance are not firm. For instance, Florida limits AFDC benefits in eight counties to twenty-four months in a sixty-month period. Florida also provides a guaranteed transitional program and continues the child's portion of the AFDC grant if it is necessary to keep the family together. In addition, Florida also excludes some individuals from time limits if they have a particular hardship, which is called a "good cause" exemption.

Like Florida, other states with time-limit waivers only impose them in a few counties, and the waivers do not apply to everybody. The states grant hardship exclusions and often continue to support children regardless of the parent's eligibility. Overall, while states seem willing to experiment with time limits on AFDC benefits, the nature of present waivers suggests states are cautious about implementing drastic measures for fear of causing family breakups and hurting children.

Another popular experiment is to discourage welfare families from having more children while receiving AFDC by setting family caps. Families only receive assistance for the children they have when they apply for benefits; children born after AFDC payment begin do not result in an increase in the AFDC check. Approximately twenty states have applied for or received a waiver to implement family caps and, as mentioned earlier, family caps are part of the Republican congressional welfare reform legislation.

Social contract provisions—or AFDC benefits in return for participation in school, work or job-training activities—are another popular waiver request. In fact, most waivers mandate some form of reciprocal action by many AFDC recipients, although usually not the entire AFDC population. For instance, the Ohio Learning, Earning, and Parenting program focuses on teen parents and provides bonuses for teen parents who attend school while reducing the AFDC grant of teens who do not attend school (a refinement of the original Wisconsin "Learnfare" project).

Other waivers require AFDC recipients to sign Self-Sufficiency Pacts (SSP), a form of contract between the individual and the state, outlining what actions the AFDC recipient will take to reduce her or his dependence on AFDC in return for specific assistance. AFDC recipients may receive job training, child care, transportation assistance, or other specialized social services. In return, they must look for jobs upon completion of the SSP and agree to a time limit on their AFDC benefits.

Missouri is presently conducting two welfare reform experiments that require waivers. The first is the 21st Century Communities demonstration project in Kansas City. The second is the Missouri Families-Mutual Responsibility Plan (MF-MRP).

Briefly, the Kansas City 21st Century Communities project, operated in conjunction with the Missouri JOBS program, attempts to create and stabilize new jobs in the Kansas City inner city by subsidizing employers who hire and train AFDC recipients. Missouri diverts the AFDC and food stamp benefits of participating AFDC individuals to the employer in order to supplement the wages paid by the employer. AFDC recipients work for an employer for up to forty-eight months, receiving a pay check from the employer during that time.

In addition, 21st Century participants retain their Medicaid card, receive supportive social services such as child care and transportation assistance if necessary, and are allowed to accumulate ten thousand dollars in assets. As stated earlier, this program is only operational in Kansas City and will support approximately three hundred individuals at any point in time.

The second of Missouri's waivers, the Missouri Families-Mutual

Responsibility Plan, requires AFDC recipients to sign self-sufficiency pacts with the state. In return for certain services such as educational assistance, job training, child care, or transportation assistance for a period of time, AFDC recipients agree to participate in good faith and eventually look for work and take a job. In addition, the AFDC recipients may accumulate additional assets, but they are subject to time limits. Beginning in 1997, any adult who has received AFDC for thirty-six months, has signed a self-sufficiency pact, and left public assistance is no longer eligible to receive assistance in the future; however, this time limit applies only to adults, and the children on the AFDC case can continue to receive assistance.

Waivers allowing states to experiment with the AFDC program provide a "bottom-up" approach to welfare reform—versus the historical "top-down" approach originating from Washington—and have become quite popular. The majority of states have applied for and received at least one. Not only do waivers provide laboratories for experimentation and innovation in the states, they also provide the opportunity to address local welfare problems with locally devised solutions.

The waiver process also fills the void created by the welfare reform gridlock occurring in Washington as both political parties, President Clinton, and Congress fight to take credit for reform of the public welfare system. Many of the ideas being proposed in both the Republican and Democrat versions of welfare reform legislation originated in the states in the form of 1115 Waivers. Had it not been for the waiver process, it is questionable whether policymakers would have as much knowledge about welfare reform experiments as presently exists. Under PRWO-96, however, states that have waivers in existence may elect to either keep them or terminate them and be held harmless for accrued federal cost liabilities.

RECENT RESEARCH FINDINGS FROM THE MANPOWER DEMONSTRATION RESEARCH CORPORATION

One of the common difficulties experienced in most evaluation projects, is determining whether a particular program outcome is the result of a specific treatment or if it occurred by chance, for reasons not related to the treatment. The desired outcome of the JOBS program and the state welfare reform experiments initiated by the 1115 Waiver process is reduced dependence on the public welfare system, as represented by decreasing state AFDC caseloads and/or smaller average AFDC grants due to greater work effort by AFDC recipients. A secondary desired outcome is greater family economic stability and a higher standard of living than that which the public welfare system provides. (See discussion in chapter 3, "The Economics of Public Assistance" and table 3-4.)

A review of the desired outcomes shows that AFDC caseloads have been declining over the past couple of years since reaching record high levels in the winter of 1994.[7] The Missouri AFDC caseload reached a record high of 92,376 cases in February 1994. In May 1996, it was 81,319, a reduction of 11,057 cases or almost 12 percent.[8] Similar reductions have been reported nationally.

The American Public Welfare Association (APWA) reported that AFDC caseloads decreased nationally by 6.42 percent from September 1994 to September 1995, with all states except Nevada, Idaho, and Hawaii experiencing decreases. AFDC caseloads in forty-one states and the District of Columbia dropped by at least 5 percent with Indiana experiencing the largest drop of 22.67 percent.[9] The May 29, 1996, issue of *USA Today* reported the number of people receiving AFDC nationwide decreased by 9 percent from January 1993 to January 1996 with Indiana again experiencing the largest decrease of 30 percent.[10]

Have the decreases nationwide been a result of the Job Opportunities and Basic Skills Training Program (JOBS) and 1115 Waiver reforms, or have the AFDC reductions been a direct result of an improved economy? An April 1995 Government Accounting Office (GAO) report, *Welfare to Work: Measuring Outcomes for JOBS Participants*, found that "very little is known nationally about the outcomes of JOBS participants because HHS has not moved aggressively on developing an outcome monitoring system."[11]

The Manpower Demonstration Research Corporation (MDRC), which has been studying state welfare-to work programs since the early 1980s, however, has been conducting a multistate evaluation of the JOBS program using an experimental design. MDRC has released recent findings that support the opinion that some state welfare reform programs are contributing to AFDC caseload decreases. In a summer 1995 article in *Public Welfare*, MDRC found mixed results in its multistate study and reported that recent data indicates "substantial variability in the success of states in implementing work-focused mandates." MDRC, however, "identified clear examples of excellence: JOBS programs that have successfully implemented participation mandates, changed the nature of welfare, and gotten many welfare recipients to substitute earnings for AFDC payments." According to MDRC, "The challenge is to learn from and build upon the more successful programs."[12]

During a briefing in Kansas City, Missouri, on June 17, 1996, MDRC reported on lessons from their research. According to MRDC President Judith Gueron:

> The GAIN—California's Greater Avenues for Independence Program—evaluation has shown that welfare-to-work programs that require participation in employment and training can increase earnings and employment, save welfare dollars, and return more to government budgets than they cost. At the same time, the programs do not eliminate the need for welfare, and many who leave welfare are still in poverty. These are incremental approaches which can balance the goals of reducing dependency and maintaining the safety net.[13]

Using an experimental design and comparing the outcomes of experimental group subjects—GAIN participants—with control group participants who were not allowed to participate in GAIN, MDRC found that the experimental group subjects' average employment and earnings increased, welfare receipt and the average welfare payment decreased, and individuals received more of their income from earnings. Other findings were that total income did not change appreciably because earnings replaced AFDC; program gains persisted for several years; and on an average, the GAIN program returned seventy-six cents for every dollar invested.[14]

For the Riverside project, the GAIN site with the best program results, however, employment rates increased by 9 to 18 percent a year; earnings grew by 50 percent, from $900 to $1,200 a year; individuals on AFDC decreased by 5 percent to 7 percent a year; average yearly welfare payments decreased by 15 percent, or $584 to $703 per year; large positive results were found for all subgroups; and the program returned $2.84 for every dollar invested.[15]

During its research, MDRC classified the welfare-to-work activities of the sites they were studying into two distinct service delivery strategies for purpose of analysis. The first strategy, identified as the Labor

Force Attachment (LFA) approach, is characterized by immediate job entry, even at low wages, and up-front job search followed by short-term education or job training, with case management and supportive services available as needed.

The second strategy, the Human Capital Development (HCD) approach, also referred to as Human Capital Investment (HCI), is characterized by providing education and job training prior to entering the job market. In this model, basic education or vocational training is followed by job search, with case management and supportive services provided as needed.

After two years of analysis, MDRC has concluded that the Labor Force Attachment (LFA) strategy produced the best short-term results and substantially reduced AFDC utilization and increased earnings. MDRC attributed AFDC savings to participants leaving welfare. According to MDRC, in JOBS sites that used an LFA strategy, AFDC caseloads decreased by 16 percent, AFDC payments decreased by 22 percent, food stamp payments decreased by 14 percent, and earnings increased as much as AFDC payments decreased. Additionally, total measured income changed little, the earnings impacts appear likely to continue, and these impacts occurred in all sites studied.[16]

In contrast, MDRC has found the Human Capital Development (HCD) approach did not have the same degree of immediate short-term impacts as did the LFA approach. The HCD strategy reduced AFDC but did not result in offsetting earnings increases. The AFDC decreases were largely a result of sanctioning—reducing AFDC grant amounts for non-cooperation. MDRC points out that the HCD concept implies the impact of education and training may be delayed, and MDRC's most recent data indicates that longer-term results may be more positive. According to MDRC, after two years of analyzing the HCD strategy, AFDC impacts were about half that demonstrated by the LFA approach, but increasing.[17]

In their study of Riverside, California, and Grand Rapids, Michigan, LFA strategies, MDRC identified key practices that seem to contribute to the success of the LFA approach. First, senior management placed a priority on the LFA strategy which filtered down and was reinforced throughout the organization. Second, the organization had a commitment to serve the entire mandatory population, not just the volunteers, and had adequate resources available to do so. Third, successful LFA sites placed an emphasis on getting people into a job quickly, even a low-paying job. Fourth, LFA staff were willing to use sanctions—grant reductions—for noncompliance and to enforce mandatory participation. Fifth, these two LFAs used a mixed service delivery strategy emphasizing job search but also providing basic education and vocational training. Sixth, it was important for LFA to have an outcome-focused orientation with placement standards for case managers. Seventh, establishing close links with private sector employers to help AFDC recipients find work was also important. Eighth, staff had to provide close monitoring of program participants with swift sanctions for noncompliance.[18]

In addition, MDRC feels it has learned several lessons from years of observing welfare-to-work programs. MDRC has found mandatory welfare-to-work activities can increase employment and earnings, and reduce welfare expenditures. Predictably, the most successful programs are funded with adequate resources. Successful programs provide mixed services, focusing on job search supported by education and job training, with participation enforced by sanctions. MDRC findings indicate it is important to require as many people as possible to participate in welfare-to-work programs; however, participation rates that are set too high can be detrimental to a good program, especially if adequate resources do not exist. MDRC notes time-limited welfare restrictions increase the importance of running mandatory programs with a strong employment focus to get people permanently employed. Further, it appears communicating new policies about work requirements, time limits, and AFDC recipient obligations are crucial if behavioral change is to occur.[19]

Overall, MDRC research came to the conclusion that welfare-to-work programs have not increased overall family income, although increased earnings tend to offset AFDC loses. Also, financial incentives, such as higher income disregard limits, can provide more income to a working family but may result in the family staying on welfare longer. The effect on welfare costs are uncertain, however, since increased work and earnings may lower monthly AFDC grants. Financial incentives appear to be more effective when combined with a strong welfare-to-work program. The two policies tend to reinforce each other.[20]

While MDRC's research has provided considerable insight about welfare-to-work programs and their effects on AFDC caseloads and costs, the findings reinforce earlier research showing that these programs, by themselves, do not move people from welfare to complete economic self-sufficiency. The most significant finding of all is that while AFDC recipients participating in these programs work more and use less AFDC, their available income remains fairly constant. They do not escape poverty.

The amount of wages they earn basically replaces the amount of AFDC they lose. In fact, great numbers of ex-AFDC families are not moving higher on the economic scale.

ENLIGHTENED SKEPTICISM

While the MDRC research efforts present positive findings about the ability of the JOBS program and other welfare reform experiments to reduce welfare caseloads, concurrently a body of welfare scholars expresses skepticism about current welfare reform efforts and the need for reform. Other scholars note that national policy goals confuse reducing welfare dependency and reducing poverty, and that strategies to attain these two goals may be convoluted and inconsistent.

For instance, in *"Ending Welfare As We Know It": Another Exercise in Symbolic Politics*, Joel Handler claims that the reform issue is not really related to the cost of AFDC, but to the perception that the "money is being spent to 'reward' young women without education or skills for bearing children out of wedlock: the subtext is that such women are inner-city, substance-abusing blacks spawning a criminal class."[21]

Handler argues that this perception is based on a stereotype of the welfare population; that "most AFDC recipients are working or trying to work, although the low skills and poor education of many often preclude work as a reasonable option; and that long-term welfare receipt is the exception, not the rule, since half of all recipients exit AFDC within one year, and about three-quarters leave within two years. However, many return, since as previous research points out, low-income/poverty families tend to mix work and wages with welfare."[22]

Handler feels current reform proposals will fail because they are based on misguided assumptions about welfare dependency, and they stigmatize the poor; moreover, they attempt to reform the recipient instead of improving the labor market and focusing on the greater problem of poverty.

Handler feels the real problem underlying welfare is poverty. He notes poverty is the single most powerful predictor of harmful behavioral consequences ascribed to welfare families—more stress and a higher incidence of child abuse and neglect. According to Handler, "Poor children are more likely to suffer from physical and mental health problems, do poorly in school, and compromise successful development by early sex, pregnancy, substance abuse, delinquency, and crime. Early school failure is one of the strongest predictors of adolescent problems, including violent behavior."[23] He believes many of the pathological characteristics attributed to the welfare population are, in fact, related to the more prevalent issue of poverty.

As a result, Handler feels the welfare reform proposals, both the Democrat and Republican, serve a primarily symbolic purpose. They treat the dependent poor (primarily single mothers) as deviants in need of moral reform. Handler recognizes that a majority of the citizenry decries welfare, and that the proposed reforms such time limits, family caps, and mandatory work requirements affirm our norms by stigmatizing others as a symbolic exercise, intended less to 'reform' the deviants than to make us feel good. According to Handler:

> The evidence is consistent that the welfare poor
> share the work ethic and that most seize opportunities
> to improve themselves and leave welfare when they
> can. None of the welfare programs, whether education, training, job search, or workfare, does anything
> to change the labor markets, and adequately paying
> jobs are becoming increasingly unavailable. Welfare
> as contrasted with "work" is simply an obsolete idea
> for most single mothers on welfare. Yet, policymakers
> and academics insist we need to send a message.[24]

Another apparent skeptic, Frederick C. Thayer, author of *The Comic Opera of Welfare Reform*, finds that approximately eight million Americans are unemployed, many of them welfare recipients. He feels that the principal players in the comic opera of reform welfare—senior policymakers and political candidates—are accusing the unemployed of such sins as laziness and promiscuity when national policy demands a certain rate of unemployment in order to slow the economy, keep inflation in check, and provide a pool of reserve workers. Thayer even suggests that President Bill Clinton has his economic advisor, Laura D'Andrea Tyson, pushing Federal Reserve Chairman Alan Greenspan to keep the unemployment rate above 6 percent by keeping interest rates high.[25]

According to Thayer, "The most recent official expression of the policy is an essay in the *New York Times* of April 15, 1994, by Laura D'Andrea Tyson, Clinton's chief economist, arguing that inflation becomes a threat when the joblessness rates falls into the range of 5.9 to 6.3

percent—roughly eight million job seekers. This eight million does not include the temporarily laid off, part-time workers who cannot find full-time work, or the discouraged—including perhaps many AFDC recipients." Thayer also points out that now 6 percent unemployment is repeatedly labeled "full employment."[26]

Thayer also blames a host of others—especially the religious right movement—for contributing to and becoming supportive cast members in the welfare reform comic opera. According to Thayer:

> The huge chorus of the unemployed is silent, dumb-founded by the biblical melody of the Evangelicals—"no work, no eat," the solemn chant of the quasiscientists—"you have inherited stupidity, and you should not have children," the plaintive weeping of the secular and religious moralists—"no sex before marriage, no matter what age," and the vocal exercise of the economists that has so much immediate influence on the public policy—"we must maintain high unemployment."[27]

Thayer argues that none of the significant questions about reforming welfare will be addressed until those preaching the gospel of reform acknowledge that welfare dependency has been created by the long-term public policy of compulsory unemployment. "Until we disentangle this country's religious and moral history that ties together sex, unemployment, and welfare, we have little chance of making significant progress on these high-profile issues of public concern."[28]

As Thayer notes:

> This comic opera resembles the tragedy staged by an earlier bipartisan affluent Washington mob that emptied the mental hospitals, chose to "forget" the community mental health centers they had promised, and left the helpless to roam the streets. This time, mothers may have to make beggars of their kids in order to avoid starvation. At that point, more speeches and books about "virtue" will doubtless follow.[29]

Logical outcomes aside, it appears the country's avowed present public policy goals are to reduce poverty, reduce AFDC dependency, reduce AFDC program costs, increase the stability and economic well-being of families, provide children with a basic level of support, revitalize American morals and the work ethic, and protect the economy from inflation. Neither the proposed Republican or Democrat welfare reform strategies have realistically identified and prioritized these policy goals nor have they identified a realistic strategy for achieving them. As often happens with the issue of welfare reform, research has been superseded by rhetoric, and ideology has replaced rational policy development.

NOTES

1. Gary Stangler, "Lifeboats vs. Safety Nets: Who Rides...Who Swims," Dollars Sense: Diverse Perspectives on Block Grants and the Personal Responsibility Act, Institute for Educational Leadership, (1995), 67–72.

2. Much of the information contained in the following section about congressional efforts to enact welfare reform legislation was obtained from telephone interviews with staff of the American Public Welfare Association in Washington, D.C.; Mark Greenberg with the Center for Law and Social Policy in Washington, D.C.; and from the following publications and documents: *U.S. Congress, H.R. 4, The Personal Responsibility and Work Opportunity Act of 1995*; *U.S. Congress, H.R. 3734, The Personal Responsibility and Work Opportunity Act of 1996*; Thomas Corbett, "Welfare Reform in the 104th Congress: Goals, Opinions, and Tradeoffs," *Focus* 17 (Summer 1995): 29–31; American Public Welfare Association, "The Personal Responsibility and Work Opportunity Act of 1995, Welfare Reform Conference Key Report—Key Provisions," Memorandum to all State Human Service Administrators, January 4, 1996; American Public Welfare Association, "House Committee and Senate Finance Committee Action on Welfare and Medicaid Reform," Memorandum to all State Human Service Administrators, June 27, 1996; Center for Law and Social Policy, "A Summary of Key Temporary Assistance for Needy Families Block Grant Provisions of H.R. 3507, The Personal Responsibility and Work Opportunity Act of 1996," Informational Report, Washington, D.C. (May 29, 1996); Center on Budget and Policy Priorities, "The New House Welfare Bill," Informational Report, Washington, D.C. (June 26, 1996).

3. Michael Wiseman, "Welfare Reform in the States: The Bush Legacy," *Focus* 15 (Spring 1993): 18–36.

4. Ibid., 18.

5. In Missouri, an AFDC recipient who starts working may disregard part of her or his income and still receive a portion of an AFDC check. For instance, they may disregard the first thirty dollars they earn and one-third of the rest of their earnings for four months; they receive a ninety dollar standard deduction to cover work expenses and may disregard child-care expenses as long as they are working. The disregarded amounts are subtracted from their AFDC grant amount, and they receive the difference as an AFDC grant. Once the amount of non-disregarded

income equals or exceeds their AFDC grant, they loose AFDC entitlement.

6. Information about existing state 1115 Waivers was obtained from Michael Wiseman, "The New State Welfare Reform Initiatives," Discussion Paper No. 1002-93, Institute for Research on Poverty, University of Wisconsin-Madison (April 1993); Michael Wiseman, "State Strategies For Welfare Reform: The Wisconsin Story," Discussion Paper No. 1066-95, Institute for Research on Poverty, University of Wisconsin-Madison (December 1995); and William M. Welch, "Shifting Welfare to the States," *USA Today*, (May 29, 1996).

7. Missouri Department of Social Services, Research and Evaluation Section, Missouri AFDC Program Statistics Table (May 13, 1996).

8. Ibid.

9. American Public Welfare Association, *Welfare to Work*, Washington, D.C., MII Publications, Inc. (February 2, 1996), 222.

10. William M. Welch, "Shifting Welfare to the States," *USA Today*, (May 29, 1996).

11. U.S. Government Accounting Office, *Welfare to Work: Measuring Outcomes for JOBS Participants* (Washington, D.C., April 1995).

12. Judith M. Gueron, "Work Programs and Welfare Reform," *Public Welfare*, American Public Welfare Association, Washington, D.C. (Summer 1995), 7–16.

13. Judith M. Gueron, "Welfare Reform: Lessons from MDRC's Research," Kansas City, Missouri, June 17, 1996, Briefing Paper, Manpower Demonstration Research Corporation, New York (June 1996), 3.

14. Ibid., 3. Also see James Riccio, Daniel Friedlander, and Stephen Freedman, "GAIN: Benefits, Costs, and Three-Year Impacts of a Welfare-to-Work Program," Manpower Demonstration Research Corporation, New York (September 1994).

15. Ibid.

16. Judith M. Gueron, Kansas City Briefing Paper, 7.

17. Judith M. Gueron, Kansas City Briefing Paper, 8.

18. Judith M. Gueron, Kansas City Briefing Paper, 10. Also see David Long, Judith M. Gueron, Robert G. Wood, Rebecca Fisher, and Veronica Fellerath, "LEAP: Three-Year Impacts of Ohio's Welfare Initiative to Improve School Attendance Among Teenage Parents," Manpower Demonstration Research Corporation, New York (April 1996).

19. Judith M. Gueron, Kansas City Briefing Paper, 17.

20. Ibid. Also see U.S. Department of Health and Human Services,

The JOBS Evaluation: Early Lessons from Seven Sites, Washington, D.C. (1994), U.S. Government Printing Office: 1994-616-355/81504.

21. Joel F. Handler, "'Ending Welfare As We Know It': Another Exercise in Symbolic Politics," Discussion Paper No. 10532-95, Institute for Research on Poverty, University of Wisconsin-Madison (January 1995). Also, Joel F. Handler, *The Poverty of Welfare Reform* (New Haven: Yale University Press, 1995).

22. Ibid., abstract page.

23. Ibid., 4.

24. Ibid., 19.

25. Frederick C. Thayer, "The Comic Opera of Welfare Reform," *Social Policy* (Spring 1995), 33–35.

26. Ibid., 35.

27. Ibid., 34.

28. Ibid., 44.

29. Ibid., 44.

VIII

Summary and Final Thoughts

From this mixed experience, it is clear that work and training programs can raise the employment and earnings of welfare recipients. They can even raise earnings enough to offset the direct and indirect costs of the programs. That is good news for voters and politicians who have pinned their hopes on work and training programs. The bad news is that the good news is not good enough.

One thing is clear. Work programs cannot be expected to boost the well-being of poor families and reduce public spending on the poor. Although many of the demonstration programs "worked," none worked miracles. The truth is that lifting welfare recipients out of poverty requires both work programs and generous transfer benefits.

Employment in today's economy does not guarantee an escape from poverty. Low-productivity, low-wage jobs abound. The nation can plausibly hope to raise the skills of the least skilled workers, including potential breadwinners who depend on welfare. But it is much harder to engineer the elimination of millions of poorly paid jobs. As long as bad jobs exist, some people will hold them. If the job holders happen to be single parents with dependent children, their families will probably be poor. These families must receive public aid in one form or another, or they will remain poor.

For the majority of America's long-term dependent poor to escape poverty, employment programs must be combined with some form of earnings supplement. Inevitably, that will cost the taxpayers money.[1]

The statement above, summarizing welfare reform in general, mirrors Missouri and much of the nation's experience with the JOBS program. The good news in Missouri is that individuals who complete the training demonstrate a marked increase in earnings. It appears that investing in "human capital," as is done in Missouri, can move AFDC recipients into good-paying jobs with a future—which for some program participants is nearly "miraculous."

At the same time, however, taxpayers and policymakers in Missouri must look at the cost of providing people with the opportunity to acquire financial independence. Providing a large number of people with a second or third chance in life is expensive—and the early results of the Missouri JOBS program confirm this. When one views the cost of taxpayer support in order to provide opportunities for people in poverty, the "inspiring" nature of JOBS success stories loses some of its appeal. Overall, the findings of this study must be interpreted in the context of conflicting values and priorities.

RESEARCH FINDINGS

Tracie, mother of three children, had been receiving some form of public assistance ever since she graduated from high school in 1988. With FUTURES assistance with child care and transportation, Tracie completed her training as an EKG technician. Her good grades (A's and B's) and her internship evaluation ("excellent") led to full-time employment as an EKG technician at a local hospital.[2]

In the preceding chapters, we have examined the theoretical and historical development of the United States' employment and training policy aimed at reducing public assistance dependency. Specifically, we have concentrated on the state of Missouri's experience implementing the federal Job Opportunities and Basic Skill Training Program, Public Law 100-485, and we have examined short-term outcomes from the first two years of the program. Our examination of this topic has yielded the following key findings.

Our inquiry into the seven research questions contained in chapters 5 and 6 discovered several interesting phenomena, including the finding that the individuals being served by JOBS appear to be "more needy" or "harder to serve" than the typical AFDC recipient. As chapter 5 indicates, JOBS participants are younger, have less work experience, started having children earlier and have more children, have received AFDC longer, and are more likely to belong to a minority group and to be female, than non-JOBS subjects. While many of the differences between the two groups were relatively minor as chapter 5 indicates, when analyzed in the aggregate, the JOBS subjects possess attributes that present greater barriers to labor force participation.

This finding is significant for two reasons. First, past programs have often been criticized for "creaming" participants or serving the "less needy." This does not appear to be the case with JOBS. Second, JOBS is serving the "more needy" with a volunteer program. Recruiting strategies used for the JOBS program have enlisted sufficient numbers of hard-to-serve individuals to satisfy federal target group requirements without necessitating mandatory participation from target group individuals. In fact, there are again as many people on the waiting list to enter JOBS as there are JOBS program slots, which appears to counter the perception that welfare recipients are basically lazy and uninterested in pursuing activities that will enable them to leave welfare.

When we examined early JOBS outcomes we also found several interesting results. We found little evidence to support the contention that JOBS participation has resulted in increased labor force participation or lower AFDC benefits, at least for the aggregate JOBS population in the first two years of the program. Intuitively, this finding makes sense considering the Missouri program design, which emphasizes education and training as opposed to direct job placement. Moreover, we found evidence that participation in job-search/job-readiness activities had the most significant positive, immediate impact on short-term increased earnings while participation in high school/GED activities had a negative impact on the short-term earnings of JOBS participants.

Also, we found little evidence to suggest that the twenty-one variables tested in our regression model—representing local economic conditions, JOBS participant characteristics, and JOBS services—provided a creditable explanation of earnings and dependency. Obviously, we excluded important variables such as individual self-esteem, degree of participant motivation, promptness, appearance, intelligence, and others that potentially have a significant impact on total earnings. Quantifying abstract individual attributes such as self-esteem, motivation, and other traits, and studying their relationship to welfare dependency, however, is an interesting area for future research, possibly within the disciplines of psychology or sociology. Such a study might be approached by interviewing caseworkers to determine the characteristics that caseworkers consider most crucial in deciding whether a client gets into the JOBS program.

On an encouraging note, we find evidence that JOBS is having a positive impact on the earnings of participants who complete the program. This finding is particularly evident in the final calendar quarter for which we had wage data, where the earned income of JOBS participants who completed training exceeded the income of the non-JOBS group. During this quarter, JOBS subjects who completed the program earned an average of $668 versus $592 for non-JOBS subjects. In contrast, JOBS subjects who completed the program and who were employed earned $1,269 during the final quarter. This finding requires additional follow-up to determine the extent of this phenomenon and whether it is sustained over time.

We also found the wage gains in the Kansas City area particularly interesting because of some early dramatic increases—after just four quarters. During the first year of the JOBS program in the Kansas City area, the average quarterly earnings of the JOBS-completed group increased from $129.19 to $898.70. Similarly, over the two-year period, the St. Louis JOBS participants increased their average quarterly earnings from $462.90 to $686.80. What makes this finding particularly interesting is the fact that the Kansas City JOBS program was designed and implemented under the guidance of an advisory committee of local private citizens.

As stated earlier in chapter 6, we believe there are at least three explanations that theoretically account for the difference in the wage gains between the two areas. First, the Kansas City economy is considerably healthier than the St. Louis economy, thus providing greater employment opportunities for JOBS graduates. Next, the Kansas City JOBS population is "less disadvantaged" than the St. Louis population; therefore, they possess fewer labor force barriers and are able to find employment sooner. And finally, the Kansas City program design, with continuing involvement and oversight by the Kansas City Advisory Committee may provide a superior JOBS service delivery strategy. Theoretically, the committee design may result in a more effective JOBS program due to its initial and continued emphasis on participants obtaining basic skills, its effective initial coordination with local social service agencies in order to maximize use of existing community resources and avoid duplication, and its concern about program results with a focus on employment-related outcomes. Again, this finding would make an interesting topic for future research.

One major surprise, as noted in chapter 6, was the extent to which the JOBS participants appear to be reducing their labor force participation in order to participate in the program. As chapter 6 indicates, the fairly consistent average quarterly earnings of the non-JOBS population significantly exceeds the earnings of the JOBS population. This phenomena may be best illustrated in Kansas City, where we have four quarters of pre-JOBS wage data. The aggregate Kansas City JOBS population earned an average of $412.58 during the third quarter of 1990, one year prior to JOBS implementation in the Kansas City area. During the first quarter of JOBS, the earnings of this population dropped to $183.20. In contrast, the quarterly earnings for the Kansas City JOBS-completed subjects dropped from $503.20 in the third quarter of 1990 (one year prior to joining the JOBS program in Kansas City) to $129.19 during the third quarter of 1991, the first JOBS quarter. As stated earlier, we believe our data support the theory that program participants are voluntarily reducing their labor force participation in order to take part in JOBS. Possibly, AFDC recipients realize they need to acquire a basic education and marketable job skills if they are to compete in the labor market and escape poverty. Thus, AFDC recipients are making a conscious decision to trade income for additional education and job skills that will hopefully provide for a "less dependent" life in the future. This phenomenon presents a compelling topic for further research.

FINDINGS RELATED TO METHODOLOGY

State and local governments maintain a variety of data on individuals in their automated administrative data bases. While these data systems were initially established to allow agencies to conduct business more effectively, they present considerable potential for social science research. Since the information on these data bases is used for determining eligibility for program benefits, the data are often very accurate, and subject to verification and audit by agency staff. In addition, the researcher may have access to much more personal/confidential individual data from agency systems than could be accurately obtained by traditional survey methodology.

The benefits of using agency data systems are obvious. For example, the cost of data collection and data manipulation can be greatly reduced; the consistency and accuracy of the data can be excellent; the data sets may include a larger number of subjects and more data elements, reducing the time required to collect and edit data; the data are often consistent between states; and agencies often maintain a lengthy data series, which provides the opportunity for ongoing longitudinal research.

There are also potential hazards in using agency administrative systems for research purposes. Confidentiality of individual data is the main concern. Agency clients often provide very personal information in order to demonstrate eligibility for a particular government service. Agencies and researchers need to insure that individual information remains confidential through written confidentiality agreements or use of a data set in which identifying information has been suppressed. This issue of confidentiality is often a major concern to agencies responsible for insuring their clients' privacy but is of little interest to researchers who are not concerned with the identity of specific study subjects, only aggregated data. The notable exceptions are research designs that necessitate contacting individuals, creating the possibility that the researcher will intrude on the subject's desire for privacy.

Another concern results from agencies competing for increasingly scarce resources to run their programs. They are concerned about misinformation being portrayed as scientific research. Therefore, the researcher needs to use caution in depicting research findings so that they accurately reflect the problem studied. We suggest ongoing communication of preliminary findings to agency staff—especially if they appear controversial. Also, if findings are controversial, the agency should be afforded an opportunity to provide its perspective.

In chapters 5 and 6, we utilized a random sample of individuals who are receiving AFDC benefits and who were not participating in JOBS as a comparison group. The characteristics and outcomes of the comparison group were contrasted with those of the experimental group, which was composed of all individuals from selected counties who had received JOBS services (see chapter 5 for an overview of our research design). The purpose for this design was to establish a benchmark from which to view the experiences and outcomes of the JOBS subjects. We acknowledge this methodological approach has its flaws and that for true experimental research, the proper way to select control and experimental groups is by random selection or random assignment. We realize our experimental group, JOBS participants, may incorporate an inherent self-selection bias simply because group members volunteered to participate in JOBS. We feel, however, the use of the comparison group was valuable in that it did provide a perspective from which to evaluate the JOBS participants' attributes and outcomes.

While we are aware some true experiments are occurring, for instance the Manpower Demonstration Research Corporation (MDRC) multistate study, we question the ethics of denying services to individuals who are eligible and entitled to them, but who happen to be randomly assigned to a group that is prohibited from receiving services because of the "luck of the draw." We question whether this type of research design is appropriate since public services are denied to people who truly need them, particularly since these services may mean the difference between poverty and economic well-being for a family.

In the first chapter, we raised questions concerning our ability to measure short-term program benefits using the key indicators of wages earned and AFDC benefits received. In chapter 6, we again raised questions about the validity of relying solely on these two indicators in the short term. Again, we caution that while these two indicators can provide useful data and can identify developing trends, they should be used with a high degree of care. Program design has a significant bearing on early program success, especially when wages earned and AFDC benefits received are key indicators of success. Programs that stress immediate job placement, such as Riverside, California's GAIN, will exhibit greater immediate wages earned. Also, fewer AFDC benefits will be utilized by program participants as wages replace AFDC. In the long run, however, we believe educational activities have a greater probability of raising individuals' skill levels so they can obtain—and retain—better-paying jobs. The most recent MDRC research supports this finding.

Overall, because the Missouri JOBS program has only been in existence since July 1, 1990, and we only had access to two years of data, we feel wages earned and AFDC benefits used should not be considered definitive indicators of program success or failure. Since the majority of JOBS participants are women, it may be particularly misleading to focus on wages earned as a chief indicator of program effectiveness since studies document that women are generally paid less than men. Yet, these two indicators can provide potentially valuable information about program outcomes when combined with other evaluative data.

PROBLEM OF LIMITED PROGRAM EVALUATION

In designing this study, it was our intention to correct what we perceived as a flaw inherent in past and present programs similar to JOBS: the lack of individual, long-term follow-up. Employment and training efforts, such as the Work Incentive Program (WIN), the Comprehensive Employment and Training Act (CETA), the Job Training Partnership Act (JTPA), and JOBS, require no participant follow-up or, at best, a short-term contact to verify that an individual is working 30–180 days after she or he completes a program. For example, JTPA regulations require a thirteen-week follow-up, with "employed at thirteen weeks" as a key performance indicator.

To correct this shortcoming, this study was designed to follow both the JOBS participants and the non-JOBS comparison group indefinitely. Staff from the Department of Social Services can continue to update the records of the sample individuals on the JOBS research data set with more recent information from the various government data systems. In addition, the Department of Social Services has been providing the JOBS data set to universities that request it for legitimate research purposes.

The availability of the Missouri JOBS data should potentially increase and enhance program evaluation in Missouri and contribute to the body of knowledge concerning the impacts of employment and training programs. Also, instead of the bureaucracy "controlling" this information, JOBS data are now available to research institutions at little or no cost, with no strings attached. We hope this innovative approach will improve the quality and diversity of the JOBS evaluations.

CONFLICTING GOALS

The opening quote for this section by Gary Burtless, a labor economist with the Brookings Institute and noted author on public welfare policy, delineates the dilemma faced by public officials: enabling people to go to work may not be any more cost-effective than keeping them on welfare. This dilemma has a long history derived from conflicting values about public assistance, and the inability of policymakers to truly define the overriding purpose of programs like AFDC and JOBS. Even though JOBS was created in an atmosphere of national consensus (see chapter 4) there seems to be a continuing goal conflict which is reflected in the designs of the various state JOBS programs.

Philosophically and practically, states are grappling with whether the goal of JOBS is to achieve short-term and possibly sustained welfare savings by forcing welfare recipients into a succession of low-wage/low-skill jobs which will do little to improve the families' economic well-being. Some state programs are being run with a minimum of resources, placing emphasis on immediate job placement and sanctions for non-cooperation. Other states, like Missouri, believe the goal of JOBS is to reduce barriers to employment so a woman can compete for a job that provides her family the opportunity for a non-poverty existence. These states have chosen to emphasize "human capital investment" in education and increased skills, along with providing support services such as child care, transportation assistance, and case management.

The short-term approach has been tried and conceded a failure in past times. Yet, there is little definitive evidence to suggest that the long-term, human-capital-investment approach will work any better to improve the lives of a significant number of individuals unless society is prepared to offer opportunities to female single parents with households. Theoretically, the long-term approach should achieve better results, and there are numerous anecdotal stories that indicate women who complete JOBS have 'been able to improve their own financial lot and their dependents' as well. In fact, recent MDRC evaluations of human-capital-investment JOBS programs are beginning to uncover more encouraging data. But the question still remains: Will the results justify the effort? Will the good news be good enough to justify the cost of continuing JOBS or the JOBS program's philosophy? At this point, with the recent passage of the Personal Responsibility and Work Opportunity Act of 1996, it appears that national policy has moved to the short-term, labor-force approach and is discouraging long-term, human-capital-investment strategies. How the states will react to implement this policy is yet to be determined.

ELECTED OFFICIALS AND POLICYMAKERS

Linda, a Stoddard county resident, came into the
FUTURES program in July of 1992. Although she had
been employed in the past as a certified nurse's aid, she

was needed at home to care for her thirty-six-year-old
husband after his quadruple by-pass heart surgery.
As her husband's condition improved, Linda decided to enter training as a legal secretary. On September 12, she achieved the first step of her training: pass-
ing the GED. With this accomplishment, Linda became
the first person from her family, including her parents,
their siblings, and their children, to receive the equivalent of a high school education.[3]

One of the questions we have been asked is to predict how this
research project will be received by elected officials, policymakers, and
the "welfare community." We feel that officials who have a basic understanding of "the welfare problem" will find little in this paper to surprise
them. The findings are consistent with research projects conducted by the
U.S. General Accounting Office and the Manpower Demonstration Research Corporation (MDRC). Even some of the more unexpected findings, such as the extent that JOBS participants appear to reduce work
effort in order to participate in JOBS, appear logical when viewed in the
context of the economic choices facing most women on welfare.

On the other hand, we see the potential for officials who are opponents of some aspects of welfare reform to look at the outcomes from this
study and claim that the JOBS program is not working, that the program
delivery system needs to be changed. It may be some consolation for
these officials to note that welfare recipients are voluntarily doing some-
thing to reduce their dependency on public assistance, that JOBS appears
to serve the "more needy" population, and that some JOBS graduates are
leaving welfare. Yet, more than likely, some officials will question the
cost-effectiveness of the program. After all, while there appears to be
some good news, the bad news is that JOBS has not performed miracles.[4]
Given this, it was likely that some officials would continue to press for
further "improvements" in the system, and one result has been the recent
passage of the Personal Responsibility and Work Opportunity Act of 1996.

For better or worse, the one thing certain is that policymakers (both
elected and nonelected) will continue to have more influence on the program than its "satisfied customers." Most decisions on funding levels,
success indicators, and long-term versus short-term approaches will continue to be made by people who have never received AFDC. After all, as
chapter 5 indicates, the majority of AFDC recipients are women. In fact,

a profile of the typical AFDC recipient in our sample indicates that approximately 98 percent are women, and the vast majority are single parents who receive little or no support from the fathers of their children. In addition, they tend to be members of racial minorities—67 percent—and most have not completed high school. Given that the majority of lawmakers are male, both at the national and state level, most decisions will continue to be made by males who have no experience as a single parent trying to head a household or as a parent trying to survive on AFDC.

Because of these facts, the success of the program in the future may be due more to the amount of awareness and understanding that it generates than to other factors, including cost-effectiveness. In the past, AFDC mothers have had few lobbyists other than some "do-good" social workers and socially prominent individuals who volunteered to advocate for their cause. One of the unanticipated results of the JOBS program has been the empowering of its clients, since women who have completed JOBS now appear to be a viable sales force for the program. Yet, it is unlikely that a relatively few individuals, who have largely been ignored by the political process in the past, will have a profound impact on the program in the future.

Few of the people we talked with during this study feel JOBS or similar programs will significantly reform the welfare system or even precipitate a major reduction in the welfare caseloads. People feel the overall "welfare problem" is too big and encompasses more than just a need for employability services such as education, job training, and job-search assistance. As stated in chapter 6, recent findings by the Manpower Demonstration Research Corporation indicate "welfare-to-work programs usually benefited AFDC clients but generally only led to modest increases in their measured income." MDRC found no evidence that welfare-to-work programs move a significant number of participants out of poverty. Recent MDRC studies have found, however, that the initial positive effects derived from these programs are being sustained over the long term.[5]

Given the above MDRC findings, the appropriate question to ask is: If the positive outcomes associated with participation in JOBS or similar programs are minimal, why should government be funding programs like JOBS? Our answer is, these programs do help some people. JOBS participants have left welfare and are capable of earning a decent living for their families. While there have been those who fail, many people have succeeded and benefited from JOBS. Without programs like JOBS, many of the most truly disadvantaged citizens in our society will have little hope of ever working their way out of poverty. They and their children face the real possibility of being relegated to membership in a permanent "underclass" and to continued alienation from mainstream society. While JOBS is not the whole solution to the problems of welfare and poverty, it appears to be a very promising part of the solution—if it survives the current epoch of reform.

THE PERSONAL RESPONSIBILITY AND WORK OPPORTUNITY ACT OF 1996

As discussed in chapter 8, the Personal Responsibility and Work Opportunity Act of 1996 (PRWO-96) repeals Titles IV-A and IV-F of the Social Security Act that created AFDC and JOBS and makes major changes to other provisions of the Social Security Act. Many public officials view this as the most sweeping change in U.S. social policy since the programs of the Great Depression.

Specifically, there are two major provisions of PRWO-96 that represent a major shift in social policy. First, PRWO-96 ends the entitlement status of AFDC or welfare for the poor. Congress has, in effect, established a five-year lifetime limit for most needy individuals to receive assistance. In addition, beginning in fiscal year 1997, Congress will give each state a block grant instead of an open-ended entitlement. States will receive a fixed amount of federal funds. Once the federal money is used up, it is the state's responsibility to use state funds to support the poor—that is, if state funds are available and politicians are willing.

The second profound policy change is the federal delegation of more decisions to the states. Although PRWO-96 contains many federal strings and conditions on how the block grant can be used, welfare policy has undergone a significant devolution from Washington to state capitals. States will have considerable latitude to design their own individualized welfare systems. For instance, while states are prohibited from using federal block grant funds to provide public assistance support to an individual for more than five years, they have the option to enact state legislation that provides support for less than five years.

Under the new law, states will also be able to reduce assistance amounts and to impose stringent work requirements as a condition of receiving assistance. Further, PRWO-96 allows states to reduce the amount of money they contribute to support the poor by 20 to 25 percent, and they may also divert up to 30 percent of their federal block grant from public assistance to other activities.

Since PRWO-96 was just recently passed and no state has yet submitted a state implementation plan to the Department of Health and Human Services, it is too early to tell what the revised state welfare systems will look like. Undoubtedly, many state systems will look a lot like they do now under the existing JOBS legislation and federal 1115 Waivers. In all likelihood, however, with less federal funding and tougher federal work-participation requirements, state employment and training programs will not provide the diversity of services to help people move off welfare, and caseloads per each case manager will be larger than they are today. Also, work and immediate job placement—the labor market attachment strategy—will replace the education and human capital development strategies previously used in many of the states.

One certain outcome is that PRWO-96 will not be the nation's last attempt at welfare reform. This issue will be on the state and national policy agenda for years to come. Already, plans are under way to correct flaws in PRWO-96 after the 1996 elections. Sources in President Clinton's administration indicate the president is planning to correct aspects of PRWO-96 that are considered particularly damaging to children and families.

While all this is happening at the national level, states will be struggling to interpret the new law, submit state plans to the federal government for approval, and enact state enabling legislation on or before July 1, 1997. The states have their work cut out for them. In the meantime, poor individuals who have relied on the present system in times of need must wait and hope for the best.

> Mary wrote the following letter to her case manager regarding her experiences in FUTURES:
>
> I just decided to drop you a few lines to thank you for caring. I know I haven't been one of your best clients, but you never gave up on me. Thanks for your note—I wanted to call you but I know I would have cried. You...have been such a great help to me.
>
> With God's help and my persistence I know I will overcome my problem...I do want a better life. Once again, thanks for the note, and most of all for caring![6]

NOTES

1.   Gary Burtless, "When Work Doesn't Work: Employment Programs for Welfare Recipients," *Brookings Review* (Spring 1992), 29.

2.   Missouri Department of Social Services, Division of Family Services, *Hearts and Stars* (October 1993).

3.   Ibid.

4.   Burtless, "When Work Doesn't Work: Employment Programs for Welfare Recipients," 26–29.

5.   Judith M. Gueron and Edward Pauly, *From Welfare to Work*, (New York: Russell Sage Foundation, 1991), 26; *Welfare to Work*, (Washington, D.C.: MII Publications, April 27, 1992), 1; and "Welfare Reform: Lessons from MDRC's Research," Briefing, Kansas City, Missouri, June 17, 1996.

6.   *Hearts and Stars* (October 1993).

Appendices

APPENDIX A: DATA ELEMENTS CONTAINED IN THE JOBS RESEARCH DATA SET

I. Income Maintenance System

1. Social Security Account Number

2. Case Department Client Number—Unique number assigned by DFS staff to each AFDC case.

3. Individual Department Client Number—Unique number assigned by DFS staff which identifies the head of an AFDC household.

*4. Case Open Date—The date the AFDC case opened (used to calculate the length of stay on AFDC).

5. Reason for Case Opening—The reason the family applied for AFDC.

6. Last Case Action—The last reportable activity that occurred for an AFDC case.

7. Case Last Action Date—The date the last reportable activity occurred.

8. Case Status—Whether the AFDC case is active, suspended, or closed.

*9. County of Residence—The county in which the AFDC family resides.

*10. Date of Birth—The date of birth of the AFDC family head.

*11. Educational Level—The highest grade completed by the AFDC family head.

*12. Race—The race of the AFDC family head.

*13. Sex—The gender of the AFDC family head.

14. Second Parent Indicator—This indicates that the individual is the second parent on the AFDC case.

*15. Work Experience—The number of months worked during the last twelve months.

16. JOBS Exemption Code—Indicates the individual is exempt from mandatory JOBS participation requirements.

17. JOBS Participation Indicator—Indicates the individual is participating in JOBS.

18. AFDC Grant Amount—The dollar amount of the most recent AFDC cash grant.

19. Monthly Gross Income—Includes income from all sources including government transfer payments.

20. Monthly Income—Monthly income adjusted for deductions and used to calculate the AFDC grant amount.

21. Income Source—Indicate the source of any reportable income.

*22. Oldest Child's Date of Birth—The date of birth of the oldest child in the AFDC family (used to calculate the parent's age when the first child was born).

*23. Number of Children—Indicates the number of children in the AFDC family.

24. Subprogram Indicator—Indicates the specific AFDC program for which the family is receiving assistance.

25. Title XIX Indicator—Indicates the family is receiving Medicaid.

26. Reason the AFDC Case Closed—Indicates the AFDC case has closed and the reason for closing.

II. JOBS Management Information System

27. Social Security Account Number

28. Target Group Indicator—Indicates the individual is a member of one of the three federally designated target groups.

29. Support Services Payment, Bus Pass—Indicates the JOBS participant is receiving a local bus pass.

30. Support Services, T.R.E.—Indicates the JOBS participant is receiving cash transportation assistance.

31. Support Services, W.R.E.—Indicates the JOBS participant is receiving work-related expenses.

*32. Component Code (1 through 8)—Indicates the type of activity component in which the JOBS participant is enrolled. It is possible to have a maximum of eight entries.

33. Component Start Date (1 through 8)—Indicates the date the JOBS participant started an activity component. It is possible to have a maximum of eight entries with each entry corresponding to a component code, see item no. 32.

34. Scheduled Component Hours (1 through 8)—Indicated the number of hours per week the JOBS participant is scheduled to participate in a component activity. It is possible to have a maximum of eight entries with each entry corresponding to a component code, see item no. 32.

35. Component End Date (1 through 8)—Indicates the date an activity component ended. It is possible to have a maximum of eight entries with each entry corresponding to a component code, see item no. 32.

36. Component End Reason (1 through 8)—Indicates the reason for the component ending. It is possible to have a maximum of eight entries with each entry corresponding to a component code, see item no. 32.

37. Occupational Code (1 through 6)—Indicates the two digit D.O.T. code, identifying the occupation entered, for JOBS participant who enter employment. The most recent six entries are retained.

38. Employment Start Date (1 through 6)—Indicates the date a JOBS participant started working. The most recent six entries are retained with

each entry corresponding to an entry in the occupational code field, see item no. 37.

39. Wage (1 through 6)—Indicates the hourly wage earned by a JOBS participant. The most recent six entries are retained with each entry corresponding to an entry in the occupational code field, see item no. 37.

40. Employment End Date (1 through 6)—Indicates the date a JOBS participant stopped working. The most recent six entries are retained with each entry corresponding to an entry in the occupational code field, see item no. 37.

41. Employment End Reason (1 through 6)—Indicates the reason a JOBS participant stopped working. The most recent six entries are retained with each entry corresponding to an entry in the occupational code field, see item no. 37.

42. Employed Before JOBS Code—Indicates the JOBS participant was employed before entering JOBS.

*43. JOBS Completion Code—Indicates the JOBS participant completed all assigned activities and left JOBS.

NOTE: * indicates the data element was used in the regression model.

APPENDIX B:
QUARTERLY JOBS EXPENDITURES,
JULY 1990 TO JUNE 1992

QUARTER	EXPENDITURES
July 1990–September 1990	$ 931,385
October 1990–December 1990	$ 995,006
January 1991–March 1991	$ 1,044,174
April 1991–June 1991	$ 1,176,596
July 1991–September 1991	$ 1,007,587
October 1991–December 1991	$ 1,732,571
January 1992–March 1992	$ 2,356,438
April 1992–June 1992	$ 2,886,790
TOTAL	$12,130,547

SOURCE: Missouri Department of Social Services, Research and Evaluation Section, *Outcome Measures Report*, December 29, 1992, page 25.

APPENDIX C:
CHI-SQUARE STATISTICS—
JOBS AND NON-JOBS SUBJECTS
BY TARGET GROUP

STATUS FREQUENCY EXPECTED PERCENT ROW PCT COL PCT	TARGET NTG	TG	TOTAL
AFDC	3238	2610	5848
	2453.7	3394.3	
	28.44	22.92	51.37
	55.37	44.63	
	67.78	39.50	
JOBS	1539	3998	5537
	2323.3	3213.7	
	13.52	35.12	48.63
	27.79	72.21	
	32.22	60.50	
TOTAL	4777	6608	11385
	41.96	58.04	100.00

NOTE: AFDC = Non-JOBS Subjects, JOBS = JOBS Subjects, TG = Target Group, NTG = Non-Target Group

STATISTICS FOR TABLE OF STATUS BY TARGET

STATISTIC	DF	VALUE	PROB
Chi-square	1	887.985	0.000
Likelihood Ratio Chi-square	1	902.936	0.000
Continuity Adj. Chi-square	1	886.853	0.000
Mantel-Haenszel Chi-square	1	887.907	0.000
Fisher's Exact Test (Left)			1.000
(Right)			0.00E+00
(2-Tail)			0.00E+00
Phi Coefficient		0.279	
Contingency Coefficient		0.269	
Cramer's V		0.279	

STATISTIC	VALUE	ASE
Gamma	0.526	0.014
Kendall's TAU-B	0.279	0.009
Stuart's TAU-C	0.276	0.009
Somers' D C/R	0.276	0.009
Somers' D R/C	0.283	0.009
Pearson Correlation	0.279	0.009
Spearman Correlation	0.279	0.009
Lambda Asymmetric C/R	0.131	0.015
Lambda Asymmetric R/C	0.251	0.013
Lambda Symmetric	0.195	0.012
Uncertainty Coefficient C/R	0.058	0.004
Uncertainty Coefficient R/C	0.057	0.004
Uncertainty Coefficient Symmetric	0.058	0.004

Bibliography

American Public Welfare Association. *Early State Experiences and Policy Issues in the Implementation of the JOBS Program: Briefing Paper for State Human Service Administrators.* Washington, D.C., 1990.

American Public Welfare Association. "The Personal Responsibility and Work Opportunity Act of 1995, Welfare Reform Conference Key Report—Key Provisions." Memorandum to all state human service administrators. Washington, D.C., January 4, 1996.

American Public Welfare Association. "House Committee and Senate Finance Committee Action on Welfare and Medicaid Reform." Memorandum to all state human service administrators. Washington, D.C., June 27, 1996.

American Public Welfare Association. *Welfare to Work.* Washington, D.C.: MII Publications, Inc., February 2, 1996.

Auletta, Kenneth. *The Underclass.* New York: Random House, 1982.

Bane, Mary Jo, and David Ellwood. "The Dynamics of Dependence and the Routes to Self-Sufficiency." *Final Report to the Department of Health and Human Services.* Cambridge, Mass.: Harvard University, Kennedy School of Government, 1983.

————, and David Ellwood. "Slipping Into and Out of Poverty: The Dynamics of Spells." *The Journal of Human Resources* (1986).

Bassi, Lauri, and Orley Ashenfelter. "The Effect of Job Creation and Training Programs on Low-Skilled Workers." *Focus* 8 (Summer 1985), 3.

Baum, Erica B. "When the Which Doctors Agree: The Family Support Act and Social Science Research." *Journal of Policy Analysis and Management* 10 (1991): 603–615.

Berlin, Sharon, and Linda Jones. "Life After Welfare: AFDC Termination Among Long-term Recipients." *Social Service Review* (September 1983).

Bergson, Abram. *Essays in Normative Economics*. Cambridge, Mass.: Harvard University Press, 1966.

Bishop, John H. "Toward More Valid Evaluations of Training Programs Serving the Disadvantaged." *Journal Of Policy Analysis and Management* 8 (1989): 209–228.

Blau, David M., and Philip K. Robins. "Labor Supply Response to Welfare Programs: A Dynamic Analysis." *Journal of Labor Economics* 4 (January 1986): 82–104.

Bumpass, Larry. "Children and Marital Disruption: A Replication and Update." *Demography* 21 (February 1984): 71–82.

Burtless, Gary. "Public Spending for the Poor: The Last Twenty Years." U.S. Department of Health and Human Services Conference on Poverty and Policy, Williamsburg, Va., December 1984.

———. "When Work Doesn't Work: Employment Programs for Welfare Recipients." *Brookings Review* (Spring 1992), 29.

———, and Robert Haveman. "Policy Lessons from Three Labor Market Experiments." *Employment and Training R&D*. The W.E. Upjohn Institute for Employment Research, 1984.

Bush, George. "State of the Union Address." Washington, D.C., January 28, 1992.

Center for Law and Social Policy. "A Summary of Key Temporary Assistance for Needy Families Block Grant Provisions of H.R. 3507, The Personal Responsibility and Work Opportunity Act of 1996." Informational Report. Washington, D.C., May 29, 1996.

Center on Budget and Policy Priorities. "The New House Welfare Bill." Informational Report. Washington, D.C., June 26, 1996.

Cochrane, Clarke E. "The Double Bind: Income Support or Welfare Dependence." *American Public Policy*. 3rd ed. New York: St. Martin's Press, 1990.

Coe, Richard D. "A Preliminary Empirical Examination of the Dynamics of Welfare Use." *Five Thousand American Families: Patterns of Economic Progress*, vol. 7, Greg J. Duncan and James N. Morgan (eds.). Ann Arbor, Mich.: Institute for Social Research, 1981.

Corbett, Thomas. "Welfare Reform in the 104th Congress: Goals, Opinions, and Tradeoffs." *Focus* 17 (Summer 1995).

Chrissinger, M.S. "Factors Affecting Employment of Welfare Mothers." *Social Work* 25 (October 1980): 52–56.

Danziger, Sheldon, and Peter Gottschalk. "The Poverty of Losing Ground." *Challenge* (May/June 1985).

Decision/Making/Information. *National Survey on Women's Issues.* McLean, Va., 1983.

Dickinson, Nancy S. "Which Welfare Strategies Work?" *Social Work* 31 (July/August 1986): 266–272.

Dror, Yehezkel. "On Becoming More of a Policy Scientist." *Policy Studies Review* 8 (August 1984): 13–19.

Duncan, Greg J., and Saul D. Hoffman. "Welfare Dynamics and Welfare Policy: Past Evidence and Future Research Directions." Presented at the Association for Public Policy Analysis and Management Conference, Washington, D.C., (October 1985).

———. "The Use and Effects of Welfare: A Survey of Recent Evidence." Paper presented at the conference on The Political Economy of the Transfer Society, Tallahassee, Fla., November 1987.

Duncan, Greg J. "Myth and Reality: The Causes and Persistence of Poverty." *Journal of Policy Analysis and Management* 4 (1985): 516–536.

Ehrenberg, Ronald G., and Robert Smith. *Modern Labor Economics: Theory and Public Policy.* Glenview, Ill.: Scott, Foresman and Company, 1985.

Eichner, Alfred S. *Post-Keynesian Economics.* White Plains, N.Y.: M.E. Sharp Inc., 1979.

Ellwood, David T. "The Origins of 'Dependency': Choices, Confidence, or Culture?" *Focus* 12 (Spring/Summer 1989): 6–13.

———. "Targeting the Would-be Long-term Recipient of AFDC: Who Should Be Served?" *Preliminary Report.* Harvard University, 1985.

———, and Lawrence Summers. "Poverty in America: Is Welfare the Answer or the Problem?" U.S. Department of Health and Human Services Conference on Poverty and Policy, Williamsburg, Va., December 1984.

Employment and Training Reporter. Manpower Information Inc. Washington, D.C. (September 27, 1989), 58–64.

Fraker, Thomas, Robert Moffitt, and Douglas Wolf. "Effective Tax Rates and Guarantees in the AFDC Program, 1967–1982." *The Journal of Human Resources* 20 (1985): 251–263.

Feldman, Allan M. *Welfare Economics and Social Choice Theory.* Boston, Mass.: Martinus Nijhoff Publishing, 1980.

Garfinkel, Irwin. "Years of Poverty, Years of Plenty: An Essay Review." *Social Service Review* (June 1985).

————. "Income-Tested Transfer Programs: Introduction and Conclusion." *Income-Tested Transfer Programs: The Case For and Against*. Institute for Research on Poverty, University of Wisconsin-Madison, IRP reprint series no. 505, 1982.

————. "Welfare Policy in America." Institute for Research on Poverty, University of Wisconsin-Madison, Discussion paper no. 847-87, October 1987.

————, and Robert Haveman. "Income Transfer Policy in America." *Handbook of Social Intervention*, edited by Edward Seidman, New York: Sage Publications Inc., 1983.

————, and Sara S. McLanahan. *Single Mothers and Their Children: A New American Dilemma?* Washington, D.C.: Urban Institute, 1986.

Glazer, Nathan. "Education and Training Programs and Poverty; or, Opening the Black Box." *Focus* 8 (Summer 1985).

Goodwin, L. *The Work Incentive (WIN) Program and Related Experience*. Washington, D.C.: U. S. Department of Labor, Employment and Training Administration, 1977.

————. *Do the Poor Want to Work?* Washington, D.C.: Brookings Institution, 1972.

Greenberg, David H., and Marvin B. Mandell. "Research Utilization in Policymaking: A Tale of Two Series (of Social Experiments)." *Journal of Policy Analysis and Management* 10 (1991): 633–656.

Greenberg, Mark H. Attorney with the Center for Law and Social Policy, Washington, D.C. Telephone interviews with author, 4 and 28 June 1996.

Gueron, Judith M. *Work Incentives for Welfare Recipients: Lessons from a Multi-State Experiment*. New York: Manpower Demonstration Research Corporation, 1986.

————. "Welfare to Work Programs: Lessons on Recent State Initiatives." *Policy Studies Review* 6 (May 1987): 733–743.

————. "Work Programs and Welfare Reform." *Public Welfare* (Summer 1995), 7–16.

————. "Welfare Reform: Lessons from MRDC's Research." Kansas City, Mo., June 17, 1996, Briefing Paper. New York: Manpower Demonstration Research Corporation, June 1996, p. 3.

————, and David Friedlander, Barbara Goldman, and David Long. "Initial Findings from the Demonstration of State Work/Welfare Initiatives." *American Economic Review* (May 1986).

————, and Edward Pauly. *From Welfare to Work*. New York: Russell Sage Foundation, 1991.

Handler Joel F. "'Ending Welfare As We Know It': Another Exercise in Symbolic Politics." Discussion paper no. 10532-95. Institute for Research on Poverty, University of Wisconsin-Madison, January 1995.

————. *The Poverty of Welfare Reform*. New Haven: Yale University Press, 1995.

Harrison, Bennett. Labor Market Structure and the Relationship Between Work and Welfare. Mimeograph. Department of Urban Studies and Planning, MIT, 1977.

————. "Work and Welfare." *Challenge* (May/June 1978), 49–54.

Haskins, Ron. "Congress Writes a Law: Research and Welfare Reform." *Journal of Policy Analysis and Management* 10 (1991): 616–632.

Hill, Martha S., and Michael Ponza. "Does Welfare Dependency Beget Dependency?" Mimeograph. Ann Arbor, Mich.: Institute for Social Research (Fall 1984).

————. "Poverty Across Generations: Is Welfare Dependency a Pathology Passed on from One Generation to the Next?" Presented at the Population Association of America Meetings, 1983.

Jencks, Christopher. Comments in *Focus* 8 (Summer 1985).

Kaus, Mickey. "The Work Ethic State." *The New Republic* (July 1986), 2–33.

Kemper, Peter, David A. Long and Craig Thornton. *Supported Work Evaluation: Final Benefit-Cost Analysis*. New York: Manpower Demonstration Research Corporation, 1981.

Kondratas, Anna S. "The Political Economy of Work-for-Welfare." *Cato Journal* 6 (Spring/Summer 1986): 229–243.

Levithan, Sar A. *Programs in Aid of the Poor*. Baltimore: The Johns Hopkins University Press, 1985.

Levey, Frank and Richard Michel. "Work for Welfare: How Much Good Will It Do?" *American Economic Review* (May 1986).

Long, David A. "The Budgetary Implications of Welfare Reform: Lessons from Four State Initiatives." *Journal of Policy Analysis and Management* 7 (1988): 295–296.

————, Judith M. Gueron, Robert G. Wood, Rebecca Fisher, and Veronica Fellerath. "LEAP: Three-Year Impacts of Ohio's Welfare Initative to Improve School Attendance Among Teenage Parents." New York: Manpower Demonstration Research Corporation, April 1996.

MacNeil/Lehrer News Hour. WNET, New York, N.Y., Show no. 4599
    (April 5, 1993).

Manpower Demonstration Research Corporation. *Interim Findings from
    the Demonstration of State Work/Welfare Initiatives.* New York:
    MDRC, 1986.

Mazmanian, Daniel A., and Jeanne Nienaber. *Can Organizations Change.*
    Washington, D.C.: The Brookings Institution, 1979.

McLanahan, Sara, Irwin Garfinkel, and Dorothy Wilson. "Family Struc-
    ture, Poverty, and the Underclass." Discussion paper no. 823-87.
    Institute for Research on Poverty, University of Wisconsin-Madi-
    son, March 1987.

Mead, Lawrence M. *Beyond Entitlement.* New York: The Free Press, 1986.

———. " Policy Studies and Political Science," *Policy Studies Review* 5
    (November 1985): 319–331.

Missouri Department of Elementary and Secondary Education. *The Lon-
    gitudinal Follow-up of 1981 High School Graduates.* Jefferson City,
    Mo., October 1987.

Missouri Department of Labor and Industrial Relations, Division of Em-
    ployment Security. *ESARS WIN Reports, Table A22.* June 30, 1990.

Missouri Department of Labor and Industrial Relations, Division of Em-
    ployment Security. *Civilian Labor Force, Employment, Unemploy-
    ment and Unemployment Rates.* October 1992.

Missouri Department of Social Services. *Outcome Measures, 1991-1992
    Report.* December 29, 1992.

Missouri Department of Social Services, Division of Family Services.
    Fiscal Year 1991 Annual Report.

Missouri Department of Social Services, Division of Family Services.
    FUTURES Monthly Management Information Report. June 30,
    1992.

Missouri Department of Social Services, Division of Family Services.
    Hearts and Stars. January 1993.

Missouri Department of Social Services, Division of Family Services.
    Hearts and Stars. October 1993.

Missouri Department of Social Services, Research and Evaluation Sec-
    tion, *Missouri AFDC Program Statistics-Table.* May 13, 1996.

Missouri Department of Social Services, Division of Family Services,
    Management Services Section. *Internal Expenditure Tracking Re-
    port, Fiscal Years 1991 and 1992.*

Missouri Department of Social Services, Division of Family Services. *FUTURES Monthly Management Information Report.* June 30, 1992.

Missouri Department of Social Services, Governor's Interagency Working Group on Adolescent Pregnancy. *Two Generations at Risk.* Jefferson City, Mo., (January 1987): 20–23.

Missouri State Social Security Commission. *Aiding Needy Persons in Missouri* (June 1939), 78–79.

Missouri State Social Security Commission. *Index of Public Assistance in Missouri,* vol. 2, 1939.

Moffitt, Robert. "Work Incentives in the AFDC System: An Analysis of the 1981 Reforms." *The American Economic Review* 76 (May 1986): 219–223.

Murray, Charles. *Losing Ground: American Social Policy, 1950–1980.* New York: Basic Books, 1984.

―――. "No, Welfare Isn't Really the Problem." *The Public Interest* 84 (Summer 1986): 3–11.

National Governors' Association. *Infoletter.* Washington, D.C., August 1986.

New York Task Force on Poverty and Welfare. *A New Social Contract: Report of the Task Force on Poverty and Welfare.* New York, 1986.

Nickson, Jack W. *Economics and Social Choice.* New York: McGraw-Hill, 1974.

Paris, David C., and James F. Reynolds. *The Logic of Political Inquiry.* New York: Longman Inc., 1983.

Peterson, Willis L. *Principles of Economics: Micro.* Homewood, Ill.: Richard D. Irwin, Inc., 1974.

Pierson, Frank C. *The Minimum Level of Employment and Public Policy.* Kalamazoo, Mich.: W.E. Upjohn Institute for Employment Research, 1980.

Plotnik, Robert. "Turnover in the AFDC Population: An Event History Analysis." *The Journal of Human Resources* 18 (1983): 65–81.

Quinney, Richard. *Class, State, and Crime.* New York: McKay, 1977.

Rector, Robert. "The Paradox of Poverty: How We Spent $3.5 Trillion Without Changing the Poverty Rate." The Heritage Lectures, no. 410. Washington, D.C.: The Heritage Foundation, 1992.

―――. "Strategies for Welfare Reform." The Heritage Lectures, no. 378. Washington, D.C.: The Heritage Foundation, 1992.

Reform Organization for Welfare and The Coalition on Human Needs. *FUTURES Survey of 100 FUTURES Participants.* St. Louis, Mo., March 1992.

Rein, Martin. *Work or Welfare?* New York: Praeger Publishers, 1974.

———, and Lee Rainwater. "Patterns of Welfare Use." *Social Service Review* (December 1978), 511–534.

Rein, Mildred. *Dilemmas of Welfare Policy: Why Work Strategies Haven't Worked.* New York: Praeger Publishers, 1982.

Reischauer, Robert D. "Welfare Reform: Will Consensus Be Enough?" *The Brookings Review* (Summer 1987), 3–8.

Report of the Task Force on Poverty and Welfare. "A New Social Contract: Rethinking the Nature and Purpose of Public Assistance," Albany, N.Y., 1986.

Riccio, James, Daniel Friedlander, and Stephen Freedman. "GAIN: Benefits, Costs, and Three-Year Impacts of a Welfare-to-Work Program." New York: Manpower Demonstration Research Corporation, September 1994.

Robins, Philip. "A Comparison of the Labor Supply Findings from Four Negative Income Tax Experiments." *The Journal of Human Resources* 20 (Fall 1985).

Rogers, Charles S. "Work Tests for Welfare Recipients: The Gap Between the Goal and the Reality." *Journal of Policy Analysis and Management* 1 (1981): 5–17.

Rovner, Julie. "Welfare Reform: The Issue That Bubbled Up from the States to Capitol Hill." *Governing* 2 (December 1988): 17–21.

Ruggles, Patricia. "Measuring Poverty." *Focus* 14 (Spring 1992): 1–9.

Sanger, M.B. *Welfare for the Poor.* New York: Academic Press, 1979.

Stangler, Gary. "Lifeboats vs. Safety Nets: Who Rides...Who Swims." Dollars Sense: Diverse Perspectives on Block Grants and the Personal Responsibility Act Institute for Educational Leadership, (1995), 67–72.

State of Washington Institute for Public Policy. *Pathways to Employment.* Olympia, Wash., May 1993.

Sugden, Robert. *The Political Economy of Public Choice.* New York: John Wiley and Sons, 1981.

Szanton, Peter L. "The Remarkable 'Quango': Knowledge, Politics, and Welfare Reform." *Journal of Policy Analysis and Management* 10 (1991): 590–602.

Thayer, Fredrick C. "The Comic Opera of Welfare Reform." *Social Policy* (Spring 1995), 33–35.

University Of Wisconsin-Madison, Institute for Research on Poverty. "Measuring the Effect of the Reagan Welfare Changes on the Work Effort and Well-Being of Single Parents," *Focus* 8 (Spring 1985): 1–8.

————. Institute for Research on Poverty, "Poverty and Policy: A Conference." *Focus* 8 (Summer 1985): 13.

U.S. Congress. *Family Support Act of 1988, Public Law 100-485.*

U.S. Congress. *The Personal Responsibility and Work Opportunity Act of 1995, H.R. 4.*

U.S. Congress. *The Personal Responsibility and Work Opportunity Reconciliation Act of 1996, Conference Agreement for H.R. 3734, Public Law 104-193.*

U.S. Department of Commerce. *Current Population Reports.* Consumer Income Series P-60, no. 175 (August 1991).

U.S. Department of Commerce, Bureau of the Census. *Population and Housing Characteristics Table 1*, 1990.

U.S. Government Accounting Office. *Welfare to Work: Measuring Outcomes for JOBS Participants.* Washington, D.C., April 1995.

U.S. Department of Health and Human Services. *The JOBS Evaluation: Early Lessons from Seven Sites.* Washington, D.C.: U.S. Government Printing Office, 1994.

U.S. Department of Health and Human Services, Administration for Children and Families. Information Memorandum no. ACF-IM-92-7, May 21, 1992.

U.S. Department of Health and Human Services, Office of the Inspector General. *State Implementation of the Family Support Act: A Management Advisory Report*, no. OAI-05-90-00720, Washington, D.C., December 1989.

U.S. Department of Health and Human Services. *Federal Register* 57, no. 31 (February 14, 1992): 5455.

U.S. Department of Health and Human Services. *Job Opportunities and Basic Skills Training Program*, 45 CFR Part 205, October 13, 1989.

U.S. Department of Health and Human Services, Social Security Administration, Office of Research and Statistics. *Proceedings: 22nd National Workshop on Welfare Research and Statistics*, San Antonio, Texas, July 1982.

U.S. Department of Health and Human Services. *Status Report: Welfare-Work Programs*. Washington, D.C., 1986.

U.S. General Accounting Office. *An Overview of the WIN Program: Its Objectives, Accomplishments, and Problems*. Washington, D.C., 1982.

U.S. General Accounting Office. *To Work: States Begin JOBS, But Fiscal and Other Problems May Impede Their Progress*, no. GAO/HRD-91-106, Washington, D.C., 1991.

———. *CWEP's Implementation Results to Date Raise Questions About the Administration's Proposed Mandatory Workfare Program*. Washington, D.C.: U. S. General Accounting Office, April 1984.

Waxman, Chaim I. *The Stigma of Poverty*. Elmsford, N.Y.: Pergamon, 1983.

Welch, William M. "Shifting Welfare to the States." *USA Today*, May 29, 1996.

Welfare to Work. Washington D.C.: MII Publications, April 27, 1992.

Williams, Walter. "Work, Wealth, and Welfare." *Society* (January/February 1986).

Wilson, William Julius. *The Truly Disadvantaged: The Inner City, The Underclass, and Public Policy*. Chicago: University of Chicago Press, 1987.

———, and Kathryn Neckerman. "Poverty and Family Structure: The Widening Gap Between Evidence and Public Policy Issues." Institute for Research on Poverty, Conference Paper, February 1985.

Wiseman, Michael. "Welfare Reform in the States: The Bush Legacy." *Focus* 15 (Spring 1993): 18–36.

———. "The New State Welfare Reform Initiatives." Discussion paper no. 1002-93, Institute for Research on Poverty, University of Wisconsin-Madison, April 1993.

———. "State Strategies for Welfare Reform: The Wisconsin Story." Discussion paper no. 1066-95, Institute for Research on Poverty, University of Wisconsin-Madison, December 1995.

Index